CARDINAL NATION

THIRD EDITION

Credits

Contributing writers and editors: Joe Hoppel, Kyle Veltrop, Dale Bye, Leslie McCarthy, Rob Rains. **Page designers:** Michael Behrens, Chris Callan, Russ Carr, Matt Kindt, Jack Kruyne, Chad Painter, Bob Parajon, Angie Pillman. **Prepress specialists:** Vern Kasal, Steve Romer, Pamela Speh. **Photo editor:** Albert Dickson. **Photo research:** Jim Meier.

Photo credits

B = Bottom T = Top L = Left R = Right M = Middle

Sporting News Archives – 5-6 (inset photos), 8L, 12, 22-23, 40T, 40B, 44-45(inset photos), 48-56, 70-71, 74-77, 79, 86, 88-90, 92, 93TR, 96, 97, 99B, 112, 113BR, 115, 120-125, 127T, 130, 131, 135-137, 144-146, 147L, 152-154, 155L, 155T, 156(3), 157T, 157BR, 158(3), 159(3), 160T, 160L, 161B, 161M, 161TR, 163TR, 164L, 184, 185, 189R, 190, 191, 200, 201, 208, 209, 218, 219, 220, 221, 223, 225, All photos in The Cardinals Chronology except as individually noted.

Michael McNamara/Sporting News – Back Cover(2), 3, 16-17, 32-33, 33, 39TR, 39M, 40-41, 256

Albert Dickson/Sporting News – Front Cover TL, 4-5, 5-6, 8R, 9, 10-11, 14BL, 18-19, 21, 28(3), 28-29, 29B, 30-31, 31(4), 36, 38 (inset), 43L, 106-107, 108(2), 109(2), 116, 117(3), 141, 143, 172L, 172R, 175T, 176T, 176L, 177(3), 178M, 178B, 182, 183, 196-197, 214-215, 215L, 252M, 252R, 253M, 253TR, 253B, 255B

Sean Gallagher/Sporting News – 7T, 34(2), 35(2), 37, 38, 39(5), 119, 149B

Robert Seale/Sporting News – 43 (inset), 118, 174M, 174R, 175L, 255M

Jay Drowns/Sporting News – 142

Paul Nisely/Sporting News – 176R

Dilip Vishwanat/Sporting News Archives – 30BL, 171B, 173, 178T, 215R, 252TR, 254B, 254TR, 254M

Ed Nessen/Sporting News Archives – 148, 173, 175B

Darren Whitley/Sporting News Archives – 171R

Rich Pilling/Sporting News Archives – Front Cover ML, 26-27, 29T, 78, 80(2), 81, 82, 151, 166(2), 167BL, 168T, 168R, 170R, 198B, 198M, 199T, 250BL, 250BR, 251B, 251T

Craig Hacker/Sporting News Archives – 82-83

Rich Pilling/MLB Photos – 85, 102-103, 104, 105, 139

Peter Newcomb – 6T, 15

Malcolm Emmons – 205

Lewis Portnoy/Spectra-Action Inc. – 14BR, 69, 133, 147R, 165M, 165BR, 167T, 167R, 168L, 169T, 170T, 186

AP/Wide World Photos – 14T, 24MB, 26R, 27T, 30TR, 39TL, 42, 43T, 98, 99TR, 99TL, 101TL, 110, 126, 127B, 149T, 181, 187, 194B, 203, 211, 214, 215, 215B, 254TL

Allied Photocolor – 44-45, 157L, 164R, 194T

Courtesy of the Butch Yatkeman family – 45R, 87, 91R, 93B, 155R

Courtesy of the St. Louis Post Dispatch – 229

Corbis/Bettmann – 94, 95(2), 100, 101TR, 111TR, 111MR, 112L, 113TL, 113ML, 113TR, 162B, 188B, 188-189, 192, 193, 195, 198TR, 199B, 204, 206, 207, 210, 213, 222, 245TL

Photo File/MLB Photos – 47, 57

NBLA/MLB Photos – 227B

Louis Requena/MLB Photos – 68, 72, 73, 128, 129, 132, 134, 160R, 161TL, 162T, 163M, 163BL, 163BR, 165BL

Photo File – Front Cover BL, 58, 59-67

Dan Donovan – 111B, 168BL, 169R, 170L, 171T

Courtesy of St. Louis Cardinals – 138, 248T

10 9 8 7 6 5 4 3 2 1

CARDINAL NATION

THIRD EDITION

Presented by

SportingNews
BOOKS

Contents

Foreword

From the very first time I put on a St. Louis Cardinals uniform, I knew I was part of something special. More than 60 years later, I still feel that way about the Cardinals, and I know I am not alone.

This is a baseball team that is built on a great tradition, one that goes back more than 100 years. When I was a rookie on the 1942 Cardinals, we had a spirit that we knew was greater than any one player. We had an attitude that there was no way we were going to lose, and we didn't.

I have seen that attitude on many great Cardinal teams over the years, and with many individual players who have gone on to Hall of Fame careers. It still means something special today to be a Cardinal, and I think all of the players understand that.

It was the feeling that Red Schoendienst and Enos Slaughter experienced—and why they became so upset and emotional when they were traded. Lou Brock and Bob Gibson had it, and so did Ozzie Smith and Mark McGwire. Albert Pujols has that feeling now. There have been so many great players on the Cardinals over the years, and each and every one of them knew how blessed they were.

St. Louis is a special town, and the fans of the Cardinals also are special. Every time I go to the ballpark, I still get a sense that I am part of a large extended family. Baseball is a religion in St. Louis. It has always been that way, and I see no reason why that will ever change.

The players understand that they have a certain responsibility when they become a Cardinal, and if they are not willing to accept that, they don't stay a Cardinal for long. They are out there to honor the tradition of the team, to respect the great players who have come before them and to set a standard for future players to follow.

There is something different about wearing a Cardinal uniform, and the different expectations of the fans who follow those players. They know the game, they understand the game, but most important, they love the game. And they love the Cardinals. You can't teach that. It has to come from the heart.

The Cardinals have had great owners over the years, from Sam Breadon to Gussie Busch to the current partners, led by Bill DeWitt. They have all understood the relationship this city has with the Cardinals, and they have accepted their responsibility of always trying to put the best team possible on the field.

Even in the years when the Cardinals didn't win, the fans stuck with them.

There is no greater rivalry in sports than the Cardinals and Cubs, and it doesn't matter if the game is at Busch Stadium or at Wrigley Field. Fans from both teams will pack the place, and it will be jumping.

I was fortunate to play for the Cardinals for 22 years, and I experienced a lot of great moments in my career. My memories of those days are special. I know how lucky I was, and a day doesn't go by when I don't appreciate everything that has happened to me.

That is the attitude all Cardinals should have. Every day they get to walk into that locker room and put on the birds-on-the-bat jersey, they should realize how lucky they are and say a special thank you to whoever was responsible for them being there.

Believe me, there is no better feeling in the world.

The Essence
of the
Cardinals

Red Schoendienst and Stan Musial have earned special places in Cardinals
ore, endearing themselves to fans with their many accomplishments on the
field and their fan-friendly approach to the game. Still, star players—and great
eams—are only a part of the storied history of the St. Louis franchise.

Part of the beauty of baseball is that you never know what's going to happen. You could see a no-hitter or a triple play. Someone could hit four home runs. The game could last 20 innings.

In the history of the St. Louis Cardinals, all of those things—and much more—have happened. But mere results, the wins and losses, the record-setting performances—they don't tell the whole history of this team.

The essence of the Cardinals, a storied National League franchise that traces its lineage to 1892, can be found in the people who have been part of the organization. Some of the most notable players in the game's history—Dizzy Dean, Frankie Frisch, Enos Slaughter, Stan Musial, Bob Gibson and Mark McGwire, to name a few—have worn the famous birds-on-the-bat logo.

The 1930s Gas House Gang is among the most celebrated teams in baseball history. Rogers Hornsby batted over .400 three times. Ozzie Smith was a Gold Glove magician, a player whose induction into the Hall of Fame in 2002 marked the 38th time that an enshrinee has had a Cardinals connection. Dennis Eckersley made it 39 in 2004.

Great players, managers and executives have helped make the Cardinals a legendary franchise—but so, too, have little-known front-office people, scouts, minor league operatives and men and women working in obscure capacities. They have labored long and hard, often without recognition, because of their love of the game.

George Kissell has worked for the Cardinals for more than 60 years—as a minor league player, manager and instructor, and as a coach on the major league level. He has spent many a night on steamy fields in St. Petersburg, Fla., Little Rock, Ark. and Johnson City, Tenn. He has helped shape the careers of countless Cardinals—from Mike Shannon to Joe Torre to Ted Simmons to Todd Zeile to Placido Polanco.

What the players learned from Kissell—and great teachers like him—was the Cardinal Way of playing baseball.

"George is a fundamental person," Simmons said. "He teaches A, B, C and D. He won't give it to you any other way. And he won't go to B until he's convinced that you understand A. As far as teaching me fundamentals and an understanding of the way the game is played, George has had more impact on me than any person I've met or known."

Added Torre: "When I got to the Cardinals and met up with George Kissell, (that's) when I found out how the game should be played. The man is tireless. He cares, that's the biggest thing. He'll yell and scream at you, but it's like your mom or

Enos Slaughter was reduced to tears in April 1954 after learning he no longer would be wearing a Cardinals uniform. Slaughter had just been traded to the New York Yankees.

dad yelling. You don't like them yelling at you, but you know they're doing it because they love you."

Although Kissell and other minor league instructors are an integral part of the essence of the Cardinals, they aren't the complete story, either.

The revolutionary farm system itself is a key component of the Cardinals' rich history —and success. Created by Branch Rickey in the 1920s, it put the Cards far ahead of other teams in the signing and development of talent. The farm chain had as many as 25 teams at one point.

Cardinals baseball means tradition—a tradition passed on not only by the skills of the players, but by word of mouth. In back yards and on front porches throughout the Midwest, South and Southwest, Cardinals games have been heard for decades over the team's far-flung radio network. The smell of barbecue has mixed with

Cardinals baseball has meant the broadcasting excellence of Jack Buck, the longtime ownership of the franchise by August A. "Gussie" Busch Jr. (middle photo, throwing out the first pitch, with son August Busch III nearby) and the presence of such Hall of Famers as Bob Gibson, Stan Musial, Red Schoendienst and Lou Brock.

the voices of France Laux, Harry Caray, Jack Buck, Mike Shannon, Joe Buck and Wayne Hagin.

The Cardinals were one of the first teams to recognize the power of radio. Through the magic of such talents as Caray and Buck, millions of listeners have been transformed into Cardinals fans.

The love of the Cardinals is handed down from generation to generation, just like grandma's diamond ring and the family Bible. Grandfathers tell what it was like watching Musial and other standout players at old Sportsman's Park. Their sons tell their children about watching Gibson and Lou Brock. This generation will tell sons and daughters about September 8, 1998, the date Big Mac pushed Roger Maris out of the record book.

This love affair does more than generate affection. It also educates, making fans in the stands and those at home appreciate such fundamental skills as advancing a runner to second base with a ground ball to the right side. Clearly, the fans' knowledge of the finer points of the game has contributed to St. Louis' billing as one of the best baseball cities in America— if not the very best.

You see it at parks and playgrounds across the city and throughout the region. Kids are wearing Jim Edmonds, Scott Rolen and Albert Pujols jerseys. In pickup games, every kid wants his team to be the Cardinals. No one wants to be the Cubs. Or the Dodgers. Or even the Yankees.

Because of their understanding and appreciation of the game, St. Louis fans cheer the deeds of both superstars and bench players. When third-string catcher Glenn Brummer stole home in a game in 1982, it was a moment to cherish. It still is. When

On game day, the 1966-through-2005 version of Busch Stadium always was awash in a sea of red.

Mike Laga hit a foul ball out of Busch Stadium in 1986—no batted ball of any kind had ever left the stadium's confines—there was a buzz in the crowd. Fans realized they had just witnessed a first.

Many of those same fans went crazy when Ozzie Smith homered in the 1985 National League Championship Series, just as Jack Buck told them to do. And the fans booed umpire Don Denkinger in the '85 World Series, even if the catcalls emanated from their living rooms.

Although particularly attached to longtime Cardinals players, St. Louis fans also hold some short-termers in high esteem—players like Cesar Cedeno, Will Clark and Larry Walker, late-season acquisitions who helped the Cards reach postseason play.

Fans have cheered Jose Oquendo, Rex Hudler, Joe McEwing and David Eckstein, not because they were extraordinary players, but because they played the game at warp speed, diving for balls, sliding headfirst. It's the Cardinal Way.

It's the way the Gas House Gang went about its business. It's the feisty Orlando Cepeda-led "El Birdos" of 1967. It's Whiteyball. It's Slaughter crying after being told he no longer would wear the birds on the bat—he had just been traded to the Yankees.

And it's St. Louis fans being plunged into grief during an awful week in June 2002 when the legendary Jack Buck and starting pitcher Darryl Kile, in the prime of his life, died over a five-day period. Then, within two months, the Cardinal family was shaken again by the loss of Slaughter and Darrell Porter.

Cardinal baseball is tradition—and a deep emotional attachment.

When pitcher Bob Shirley joined the Cardinals in a trade from San Diego after the 1980 season, he sized up the difference in atmospheres. "Here, tradition is Stan Musial and Bob Gibson and Lou Brock walking into the clubhouse," he said. "In San Diego, it

"**This town has such a rich baseball history, you can't help but be caught up in it.**"

—Ozzie Smith

was (former Padres star) Nate Colbert trying to sell you a used car."

The tradition was what McGwire noticed and quickly came to appreciate after he arrived from Oakland. Edmonds sensed it, too. And young guys like Albert Pujols and Yadier Molina feel it as well.

"It wasn't until I got to St. Louis that I really got to know and understand the passion fans here have for baseball," McGwire said. "When the baseball season starts in St. Louis, they bleed (Cardinal) red. Everybody told me I'd love St. Louis, and no wonder."

Smith, the Cardinals' newest Hall of Famer and one of St. Louis' most-loved citizens, understands exactly what McGwire means.

"This town has such a rich baseball history, you can't help but be caught up in it," Smith said during his playing days. "They're all here, all the great ones. Musial, (Marty) Marion, (Red) Schoendienst, Gibson. They're people you see all the time, people you can reach out and touch. And the memories of others, like the Deans, are still here, too.

"Everything here seems to come full circle back to the ballpark. I feel I'm part of, well, a common cause."

That cause is St. Louis Cardinals baseball.

With the franchise's standout players clearly on a pedestal, ballpark-bound fans over the years have stolen a look at the statues of Lou Brock and other notable Cardinals.

The BALLPARKS

1960s

In 1966, the Cardinals moved downtown from their western outpost on Grand Avenue and baseball in St. Louis would never be the same. Busch Memorial Stadium made its debut on May 12, 1966, with the Cardinals defeating the Atlanta Braves.

The new facility actually was the second stadium named for August A. Busch Jr., longtime chairman of Anheuser-Busch Inc. Sportsman's Park, the Cards' home field from mid-1920 to May 1966, was renamed Busch Stadium in 1953 after the brewery purchased both the Cardinals franchise and the ballpark.

The centerpiece of St. Louis' downtown redevelopment, Busch

First game: May 12, 1966. The Cardinals defeated Atlanta, 4-3, in 12 innings. The Braves' Gary Geiger collected the first hit in the new ballpark, St. Louis' Jerry Buchek scored the first run and Atlanta's Felipe Alou hit the first home run.

The N.L. prevailed, 2-1, in the truly hotly contested 1966 All-Star Game. The game was played in 105-degree heat and went 10 innings. More than 100 fans required medical attention because of the conditions.

Orlando Cepeda thrilled the crowd on June 9, 1967, with the first inside-the-park home run at Busch Memorial Stadium.

Mike Shannon moved to third base in 1967 to accommodate the arrival of Roger Maris. Shannon quickly learned the nuances of the position and became a fan favorite. Hit a home run off Boston's Gary Bell that was the key to victory in Game 3 of the '67 World Series.

Catcher Tim McCarver had his best season in 1967 with career highs in batting average (.295), homers (14) and RBIs (69). He finished second in the MVP balloting to teammate Orlando Cepeda.

Bob Gibson dominated on the mound, fashioning a record 1.12 ERA in 1968. His 17-strikeout performance in Game 1 of the '68 World Series ranks as one of the all-time-great moments in Cardinals history.

Memorial Stadium was a "cookie cutter" multipurpose stadium—one of many that would dot the U.S. sports landscape from the 1960s through the 1980s. Ninety-six arches around the top of the structure blended in with the city's 630-foot Gateway Arch (visible beyond left field), adding some character to the structure.

At the stadium's debut, the infield was natural grass and would remain so until replaced by artificial turf in 1970. The field was big:

330 feet down the line in left and right field, 414 feet to dead center and 386 to the power alleys.

The stadium's most popular feature was unveiled on August 4, 1968, when a tall bronze statue of Stan Musial was dedicated on the northeast section of the complex. From that day on, "Baseball's Perfect Warrior, Baseball's Perfect Knight" provided Cardinal Nation a meeting place before games.

On September 28, 1966, lefthander Larry Jaster shut out the defending World Series champion Dodgers for the fifth consecutive time that season.

Roger Maris manned right field for the Cardinals in 1967 and 1968. In the 1967 World Series, he contributed a .385 batting average and seven RBIs against the Red Sox.

In a game against the Mets on September 15, 1969, Steve Carlton struck out 19 batters—and lost, 4-3. Ron Swoboda's two home runs drove in all of New York's runs.

A line drive off the bat of Pittsburgh's Roberto Clemente broke Bob Gibson's leg on July 15, 1967.

Center fielder Curt Flood misjudged Jim Northrup's fly ball, opening the gates to Detroit's victory in Game 7 of the 1968 World Series.

Second base was Julian Javier's home in the 1960s. Javier holds the Cardinals record for most games played at that position.

First base was the roosting place of Orlando "Cha-Cha" Cepeda, who in 1967 was N.L. MVP and cheerleader for the World Series-winning "El Birdos." Cepeda batted .325 with 25 home runs and 111 RBIs in '67.

1970s
1970-79

When the 1970s dawned, so did the era of the Busch Stadium carpet. AstroTurf was installed in 1970, thanks to a local company named Monsanto. As for the stadium dimensions, it seemed no one could decide. The center field fence was moved four times in the decade, from 414 feet to 410 in 1971, back to 414 in '72, in to 404 in '73, then back to 414 in '77 (where it would stay until 1992). Power alleys were moved from 386 feet to 376 in '73 and then back to 386 in '77.

Ken Reitz, the "Zamboni," was another fan favorite at third base. In 1977, he set an N.L. record for fewest errors by a third baseman, nine. (In 1980, he broke that mark with eight.)

Outfielder Bake McBride was named N.L. Rookie of the Year in 1974 after hitting .309 with 30 stolen bases.

In 1979, shortstop Garry Templeton became the first player in major league history to collect 100 hits from each side of the plate, getting 100 righthanded and 111 lefthanded.

Third base was the full-time home of Joe Torre in 1971. Torre won the N.L. batting title that year with a .363 average and led the league with 137 RBIs and 230 hits. He also had 24 homers.

The Mad Hungarian, Al Hrabosky, psyched himself up, then stormed to the rubber to face a hitter in the late innings. His 22 saves earned him N.L. Fireman of the Year honors in 1975.

Simba ruled here. Ted Simmons set franchise season records for homers (26 in 1979) and RBIs (96, 1972) by a catcher. And he caught more games, 1,440, than any other Cardinal.

Lou Brock set the single-season major league record for stolen bases on September 10, 1974, swiping Nos. 104 and 105 en route to 118 (a record that would stand for eight years).

Brock collected career hit No. 3,000 off Cubs pitcher Dennis Lamp on August 13, 1979.

The team on the field reflected the indecision. Sure, there were holdovers from the previous decade—such fan favorites as Lou Brock and Bob Gibson—but the Cardinals were entering a disappointing period. They nonetheless twice contended for division titles. In 1973, St. Louis rebounded from a 3-16 start and surged atop the N.L. East by the All-Star break, only to finish 1½ games behind the 82-79 Mets in a five-team race that no one seemed worthy enough to win; in 1974, the club again wound up 1½ games out of first place, this time behind the Pirates. Mostly, though, the decade was known for polyester uniforms and individual accomplishments, with fans thrilling to "Lou! Lou! Lou!" and guys like Reitz, Hernandez and Hrabosky.

Roger Freed, in perhaps his only highlight as a Cardinal, hit a pinch grand slam with two out in the 11th inning of a May 1, 1979, game against Houston, giving the Cardinals a 7-6 victory.

Vern Rapp, who took over as manager in 1977, tried to regulate the amount of facial hair his players wore.

Bob Forsch, fresh off a 20-win season in 1977, threw a no-hitter on April 16, 1978, a 5-0 victory over the Phillies.

Bob Gibson notched his 3,000th career strikeout against the Reds' Cesar Geronimo on July 17, 1974.

First baseman Keith Hernandez won five consecutive Gold Gloves as a Cardinal. Hernandez shared the 1979 N.L. MVP award with Pittsburgh's Willie Stargell, hitting .344 and knocking in 105 runs.

The decade would see a name change and an attitude change. First, the name change: The stadium would become Busch Stadium, dropping "Memorial" in 1982. Thankfully, there was no fiddling with the dimensions. Whitey Herzog knew the kind of house he lived in, and he set out to build a team that would thrive in it—one built on speed, defense and pitching.

Herzog, as general manager and manager, obtained young,

The NFL's Cardinals relocated to Arizona after the 1987 season, leaving the baseball Cardinals as the stadium's only tenant.

On September 15, 1986, Mike Laga hit the only ball ever to leave the park in Busch's 40-season history. A foul drive against the Mets, it sailed out of the stadium on the first base side approximately two-thirds of the way down the line.

Third baseman Terry Pendleton arrived with a bang in 1984, batting .324 in 67 games and showing prowess defensively.

Disgruntled Garry Templeton made obscene gestures to a matinee crowd on August 26, 1981. For the misdeed, he was fined $5,000 and suspended by G.M./manager Whitey Herzog. Templeton didn't play again until September 15. He was traded the next offseason for fielding sensation Ozzie Smith, a notoriously poor hitter at that point in his career.

Bob Forsch pitched the second no-hitter of his career on September 26, 1983, a 3-0 triumph over the Expos.

Ozzie Smith's first left-handed homer as a major leaguer shocked the Dodgers and won Game 5 of the 1985 NLCS.

Smith was without equal at shortstop, winning 11 straight Gold Gloves as a Cardinal.

Lead-footed reserve catcher Glenn Brummer made a gleeful, game-winning steal of home with two out in the 12th inning of an August 22, 1982, game against the Giants.

Bruce Sutter struck out Milwaukee's Gorman Thomas to end Game 7 of the 1982 World Series.

aggressive speedsters who could take advantage of the turf and scratch out a run or two or three. He also latched on to players known for their defense and obtained pitchers who made the most of cavernous Busch Stadium.

The fans loved it. They were rewarded in 1982 with St. Louis' first World Series championship in 15 years, followed by pennant-winning teams in 1985 and 1987. New stars played their way into fans' hearts—Smith, Sutter, Coleman, Tudor and McGee. And new rivals and adversaries were born—the Mets, the Twins and umpire Don Denkinger. Cardinal Nation loved the '80s.

The automatic tarpaulin ran over Vince Coleman's leg before Game 4 of the 1985 NLCS, knocking Coleman out of the rest of the postseason. The speedster captured the N.L. Rookie of the Year award that year with a 110-steal season.

Jack Clark provided power for St. Louis' N.L. champions of 1985 and '87, hitting 57 homers and driving in 193 runs for those clubs.

Willie McGee won the N.L. MVP award in 1985, leading the league with a .353 batting mark.

On August 4, 1986, Ozzie Smith made arguably his most spectacular acrobatic play. He raced into outfield and, with his back to the plate, caught a short fly ball hit by the Phillies' Von Hayes by diving over a sliding Curt Ford (St. Louis' left fielder).

Popular Tommy Herr anchored second base in the 1980s. In 1985, he batted .302 and finished third in the N.L. in RBIs with 110 despite hitting only eight homers.

Joaquin Andujar won 15 games for the 1982 World Series champion Cards and 21 for the 1985 pennant-winning club. He led the N.L. with 20 wins in 1984.

After a 1-7 start in 1985, John Tudor won 20 of his last 21 decisions. He tossed 10 shutouts. The lefthander won two games in the '85 World Series.

Todd Worrell was selected N.L. Rookie of the Year in 1986 after recording 36 saves and a 2.08 ERA.

1990s
1990-99

The decade started ominously in 1990 when the Cardinals finished in last place for the first time since 1918. "Whiteyball" came to end on July 6 of that year, with Whitey Herzog resigning as manager of a Cards team that was on the bottom of the N.L. East. The Joe Torre era started in August. The first half of the 1990s was marred by a players strike that canceled the 1994 World Series and reduced the length of the 1995 season, but it also featured the 100th anniversary of the storied Cardinals franchise in 1992.

Where McGwire's 545-foot blast off the Marlins' Livan Hernandez dented the *St. Louis Post-Dispatch* sign in dead center field on May 16, 1998.

Landing areas for McGwire's historic 62nd and 70th home runs during the 1998 season.

Mark McGwire endeared himself to Cardinals fans when he signed a three-year contract on September 16, 1997. That night, he hit a 517-foot homer at Busch Stadium— the longest, at the time, in the ballpark's history.

Shortstop Edgar Renteria had a big impact in his first season with the Cardinals, leading the 1999 club in games (154), hits (161), doubles (36) and steals (37).

J.D. Drew made his big-league debut on September 8, 1998. Oh, and there was something else of note going on that night ...

McGwire embraced his son Matt after breaking Roger Maris' single-season homer record on September 8, 1998.

By the end of the decade, the team's fortunes had turned around, thanks to a new ownership group and the presence of general manager Walt Jocketty and manager Tony La Russa.

The look of Busch Stadium changed, too. With the football configuration no longer necessary, the bullpens were placed beyond the outfield walls, a picnic area and other fan-friendly features were added to the mix and a retro-type scoreboard was introduced.

On the field, the turf was pulled up in favor of grass. Despite reasonable dimensions (402 to center field and 372 to the power alleys), Busch Stadium couldn't shake its reputation as a pitchers park—until, that is, the Cardinals obtained Mark McGwire in a trade on July 31, 1997. His arrival changed everything.

McGwire hit career homer No. 500 on August 5, 1999. He followed up his record-breaking 1998 season with 65 homers in '99.

The Cardinals made their first postseason appearance in nine years in 1996 and were on the brink of reaching the World Series when Brian Jordan's eighth-inning homer in Game 4 of the NLCS thrust St. Louis into a three-games-to-one lead over Atlanta. The Cards' hopes were dashed, though, when the Braves won the next three games.

Lee Smith set a then-N.L. record for saves with 47 in 1991.

The "Secret Weapon," Jose Oquendo, set major league records for a second base-man in 1990 with a .996 fielding percentage and only three errors.

Ozzie Smith said goodbye on September 29, 1996, playing his last regular-season game.

On September 17, 2001, broadcaster Jack Buck soothed a grieving nation. After six days of inactivity following the terrorist attacks on the United States, major league baseball resumed play that night and Buck read a poem at Busch—one he penned himself. His voice cracked with emotion.

Matt Morris won 22 games in 2001, the most victories by a Cardinals pitcher since Bob Gibson won 23 in 1970.

In 2003, Mike Matheny became only the third catcher in major league history (100 or more games) to have an errorless season.

Scott Rolen became a stalwart at third base after being acquired in a July 29, 2002, trade with the Phillies. Rolen, shortstop Edgar Renteria, second baseman Fernando Vina and center fielder Jim Edmonds all won Gold Gloves in '02.

Only once in the first six seasons of this decade did the Cardinals fail to make the playoffs. It was a time of titles and trauma—fans celebrated four outright N.L. Central championships, one tie for the division crown and one pennant, but they also said goodbye to beloved broadcaster Jack Buck and pitcher Darryl Kile.

As Busch Stadium remained intact, other ballparks fell to the wrecking ball. Baseball-only "retro" facilities were the rage as new stadiums sprung up across the country, and it became clear to St. Louis' ownership group that in order to keep a competitive team on the field, a new stadium was needed for the Cardinals, too.

But Busch Stadium did not go quietly.

Memorial services for broadcaster Jack Buck and pitcher Darryl Kile were held at Busch Stadium just days apart in 2002. Buck died June 18 after battling a long illness; Kile was found dead of a heart ailment on June 22 in a Chicago hotel room hours before the team was to play the Cubs.

On April 5, 2004, President George W. Bush threw out the ceremonial first pitch on opening day at Busch Stadium. Wearing a Cardinals jacket, he fired a strike.

Center fielder Jim Edmonds made a momentum-changing catch in Game 7 of the 2004 NLCS, helping St. Louis defeat the Astros and reach the World Series for the first time in 17 years. That the Cards were even playing a Game 7 was due to Edmonds' heroics the night before—he hit a game-winning home run in the 12th inning.

In 2001, Albert Pujols, ticketed for the minor leagues, made the roster out of spring training. He hit a home run in his Busch Stadium debut and went on to win N.L. Rookie of the Year honors with a .329 average, 37 HRs and 130 RBIs.

Will Clark's performance after being obtained from the Orioles on July 31, 2000, electrified the Cardinals and their fans. In 51 games, he batted .345 with 12 home runs and 42 RBIs and helped St. Louis into the playoffs.

So long, old friend

Busch Stadium often was derided for its "cookie cutter" design, for being a mass of concrete possessing little charm. But to the millions of Cardinals fans who poured into its seats for 40 seasons, Busch Stadium was a special place where magic happened.

Busch was where championships were won, where memories were formed and then frozen. It was where Bob Gibson closed his career, where Lou Brock and Mark McGwire set records, where Ozzie hit that home run. It was where families went for a little fun and where an old friend, Jack Buck, went to work.

In 2005, the stadium opened its turnstiles for the final time to the "sea of red." The final home opener featured the heroes of Cardinal Nation returning as National League champions. The final season featured Chris Carpenter smoking the corners of the plate, Albert Pujols lacing balls over the wall, Jim Edmonds tracking down potential extra-base hits in the gap. In its final days—even as construction cranes working on the new stadium peered over it—old Busch showed it still had plenty of life.

Dwindling numbers

Once the first pitch of the 2005 home opener was thrown, the countdown was on to the final regular-season game at Busch Stadium. During each game, a notable figure who usually had a strong tie to St. Louis' sports history peeled off a number on the right field wall to reveal how many home contests remained. Some of the notables chosen to make the countdown:

No. 81, Jackie Smith. The former football Cardinals tight end. Other people with St. Louis football ties who peeled off numbers were Isaac Bruce (No. 80) of the Rams and Jim Otis (35), Roger Wehrli (22) and Jim Hart (17) of the old football Cardinals.

No. 76, Ted Simmons. Perhaps the greatest Cardinals catcher ever.

No. 66, Bob Pettit. One of the NBA's 50 greatest players of all-time.

No. 57, Flynn, Kannon and Sierra Kile. The wife and children of Cardinals pitcher Darryl Kile, who died in 2002. Kannon also served as the batboy for that night's win over the Nationals.

No. 50, Joe Torre. The current Yankees manager and former St. Louis player and manager was the N.L. MVP as a Cardinal in 1971.

No. 45, Bob Gibson. Hall of Famer who is widely regarded as the greatest Cardinals pitcher.

No. 42, Bruce Sutter. Former star closer who recorded the final out of the Cardinals' World Series championship in 1982.

No. 31, Bob Forsch. A Cardinal from 1974-88, he's the only pitcher in team history to throw two no-hitters.

No. 24, Whitey Herzog. Managed the Cardinals to their last World Series title in 1982 and also directed the team to two other Series appearances.

No. 20, Lou Brock. Hall of Famer who once held the majors' single-season and career stolen base records and is a member of the 3,000-hit club.

No. 18, Mike Shannon. The first Cardinal to hit a home run in Busch Stadium and a team broadcaster since 1972.

No. 14, Carol, **Julie** and **Joe Buck.** In honor of husband and father **Jack Buck**, the Cardinals' Hall of Fame broadcaster.

No. 10, Tony La Russa. No. 3 on the all-time managerial victory list and winding up his 10th season as Cardinals manager.

No. 6, Stan Musial. Mr. Cardinal, Stan "The Man," the seven-time N.L. batting champion.

No. 5, Albert Pujols. A threat to surpass Musial's wondrous accomplishments in a St. Louis uniform.

No. 3, Mark McGwire. The man who captivated the baseball world with 70 home runs in 1998 and 65 in 1999.

No. 2, Red Schoendienst. Longtime favorite as a Cardinals player and manager.

No. 1, Ozzie Smith. The crowd-pleasing, electrifying Wizard, perhaps the most popular player in St. Louis sports history.

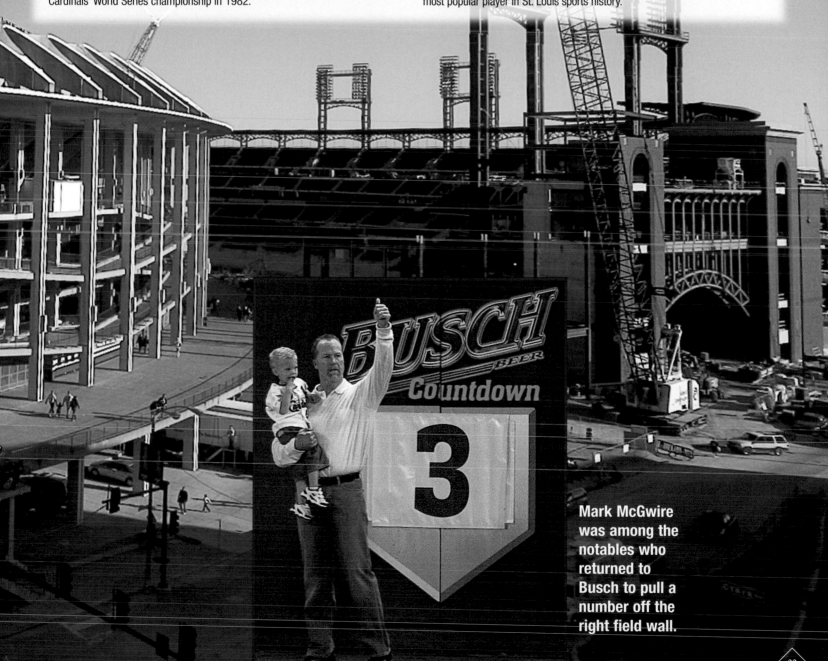

Mark McGwire was among the notables who returned to Busch to pull a number off the right field wall.

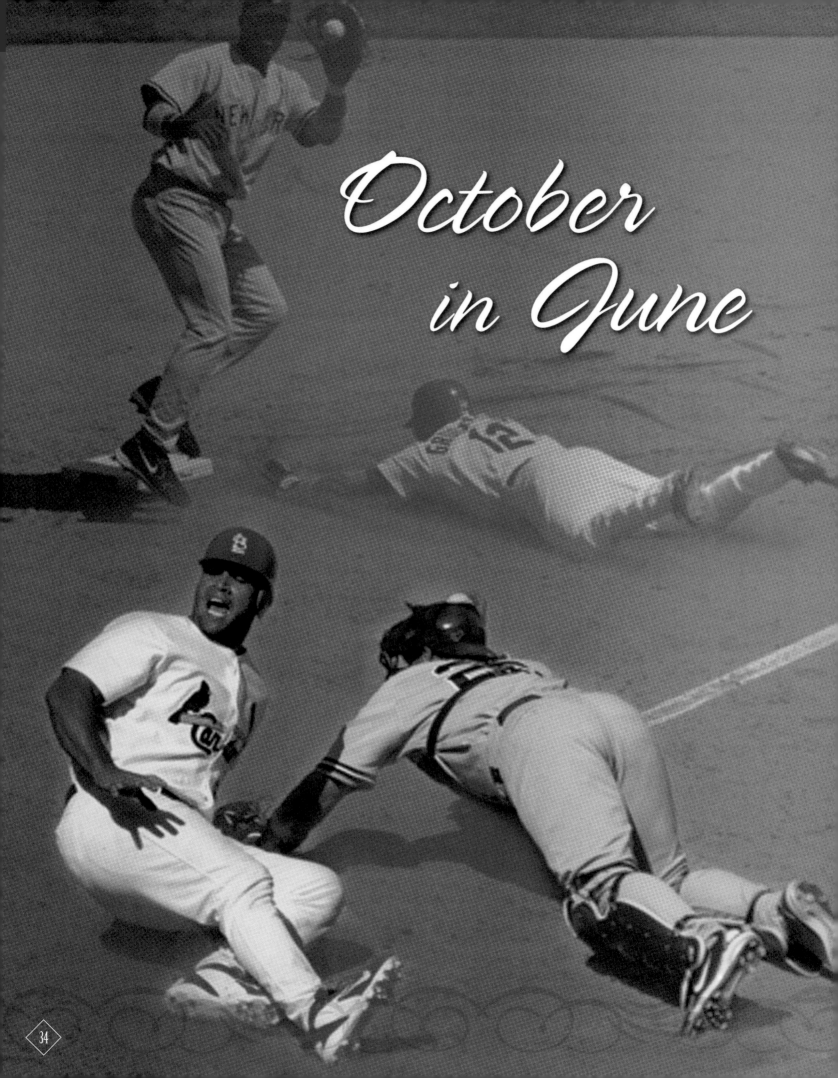

October
in June

When Cardinals fans picked up the 2005 schedule before the season, it's likely that one week popped out: June 6-12, Red Sox and Yankees, Busch Stadium. Even opponents of interleague play had to perk up at the thought of the American League's royalty visiting for consecutive series. And the action on the field lived up to the hype off it.

The Cardinals gained at least a small measure of redemption by taking two of three from the Red Sox, who had swept St. Louis in the World Series the previous October. In the opener, 50,000-plus saw Matt Morris control the Red Sox in a complete-game win, 7-1. The next game featured five hit batters and hot tempers, but the Cardinals' hot batters were the real story, as the team cranked out seven runs in the game's first three innings and rolled to a 9-2 victory. In the series finale, David Wells shut down the Cardinals and the Red Sox avoided a sweep.

Whereas Boston had visited Busch only months before, the Yankees never had. The only organization with more World Series titles than the Cardinals, the Yankees played anything like champions in the series opener, committing three errors, playing with little crispness and losing, 8-1.

Much of the hoopla surrounding this series centered on the return of Yankees manager Joe Torre, a former MVP with the Cardinals who also managed the club from 1990-95. Torre took down the No. 50 off the Busch Stadium wall during the second game and also got something he didn't get enough of when he man-

aged the Cardinals: a dominant pitching performance. Randy Johnson threw seven shutout innings and the Yankees won, 5-0.

It also appeared that the Yankees would take the rubber game, holding a 2-1 lead entering the bottom of the seventh. But Scott Seabol hit a two-run pinch homer to give the Cardinals a lead they wouldn't relinquish. It was the career highlight to date for Seabol, a 30-year-old rookie and longtime Yankees farmhand. It was a fitting finish to a special week at Busch. Beating the Red Sox or the Yankees in a series in October would provide the ultimate satisfaction for Cardinal Nation—but doing it in June felt pretty good, too.

The Cardinals ruled when the royalty of the American League came to town. After taking two of three from the Red Sox (Boston's victory was courtesy of David Wells, left), St. Louis also won the series against manager Joe Torre's Yankees.

Master Carpenter

Cardinals starting pitchers averaged 5⅓ innings in the team's 15 postseason games in 2004. And in three of the four consecutive World Series losses to the Red Sox, the St. Louis starter didn't make it through five innings. That playoff rotation, however, didn't include Chris Carpenter, who was injured, or Mark Mulder, who then was a member of the A's. And Matt Morris was pitching with a bum shoulder that required offseason surgery. But with Carpenter, Mulder and Morris serving as the top three starters for most of 2005 and Jeff Suppan finishing the year in strong fashion, the rotation served as the foundation for a Cardinals team that forged the majors' best record for the second straight season.

Mulder, the key offseason acquisition, provided a steadying presence—and a lefthanded one, at that. Just as he did in the four previous seasons in Oakland, Mulder reached the 15-win mark (he wound up 16-8).

His 10-inning, 1-0 win in April over the Astros and Roger Clemens was one of the signature games of the season. And while Morris (14 victories) no longer could dominate hitters like he did in 2001-02, he gave his team an excellent shot at winning nearly every game he started, and the same could be said of Suppan (16-10 overall, with a 1.93 ERA in September).

Carpenter, meanwhile, put on the most dominant display of pitching by a Cardinals starter since John Tudor in 1985. Starting in mid-June, the team won 17 consecutive games that Carpenter started, and he ranked among the league leaders in every major pitching category. Winner of 21 games, he used his impeccable control to get ahead of hitters, then his nasty stuff to put them away. Carpenter was so good in the first half of the year that he became the first Cardinals pitcher to start an All-Star Game since Rick Wise in 1973. And he was even better for most of the second half of the season.

Invaluable Pujols

People expect **HUGE** things from him because that's what he usually delivers.

Midway through the 2005 season, manager Tony La Russa became mystified by a question he had heard once too often: "What's wrong with Albert Pujols?" Though Pujols consistently ranked among the N.L. leaders in runs, batting average, home runs and RBIs, some observers wanted more—a monster hot streak during which he carried the team for a week or more. "I think he should get credit for being consistent every at-bat from April to now," La Russa told reporters shortly after the All-Star break. "His numbers have been really, really good and it's irritating to listen to people say, 'What's wrong with Albert?' So he does it every day as opposed to being hot for 10 days and then cooling off for five."

That, simply, is the type of standard Pujols has set for himself: People expect huge things from

him, because that's what he usually delivers. And he was exactly what the Cardinals needed in 2005: a rock who supplied a middle-of-the order presence in a lineup with many moving parts. With Larry Walker, Scott Rolen and Reggie Sanders missing significant time, and with Jim Edmonds having what for him was a down season, opponents were able to pitch around Pujols more than ever before. Yet, he produced numbers (.330 average, 41 home runs, 117 RBIs) that had him among the front-runners for the MVP award. And then he hit that absolutely electrifying home run at Houston in Game 5 of the NLCS to keep the Cardinals' hopes alive.

What's wrong with Albert Pujols?

The answer in 2005 was the same as in his previous four seasons in the big leagues: nothing.

Two hits up the middle ...

To soothe concerns over the offseason losses of shortstop Edgar Renteria and second baseman Tony Womack, Cardinals management had a singular statement to fans: Wait till you see the new guys. And sure enough, it didn't take long for shortstop David Eckstein and second baseman Mark Grudzielanek to be accepted wholly by Cardinal Nation.

Eckstein likes to make pitchers work; Grudzielanek prefers to hack at anything close to the plate. Their different plate approaches aside, the two were viewed almost in a singular fashion, a pair of baseball grinders who spray hits and play hard. Fittingly, perhaps, they finished with the same .294 batting average.

Eckstein, who played in his first All-Star Game in 2005, gave the Cardinals a legitimate leadoff hitter. Despite his 5-7 frame and unorthodox throwing motion, Eckstein got the job done defensively, positioning himself well and taking efficient routes to the ball.

Grudzielanek flashed better-than-advertised leather and showed a strong arm and good range.

Grudzielanek and Eckstein had single-game performances at Busch that will go down in franchise lore.

On April 27 against the Brewers, Grudzielanek became the first Cardinals player to hit for the cycle since John Mabry in 1996 and the first Cardinal to do so at Busch Stadium since Ray Lankford in '91. Grudzielanek homered in the first inning, singled in the second and doubled in the fourth. In the sixth, on an 0-2 pitch, he shot a ball down the right field line, completing the cycle by sliding into third.

Then on August 7, the Cardinals went into the bottom of the ninth trailing the Braves, 3-1. Abraham Nunez and So Taguchi led off the inning with singles, before Hector Luna singled off Braves closer Chris Reitsma's glove. One out later, Eckstein delivered the first walk-off grand slam at Busch since 1987, when a Tommy Herr blast beat the Mets. Eckstein was mobbed by his teammates as he reached home plate, in what might have been the most memorable scene of an unforgettable final season at Busch.

... and a flock of fill-ins

Abraham Nunez wasn't guaranteed a spot with the Cardinals in spring training, yet he ended up playing third base on a regular basis for St. Louis. So Taguchi went from a bench role to frequently hitting in the middle of the order. John Rodriguez came from nowhere to provide some pop. And there also were contributions from the likes of John Mabry, Hector Luna, Scott Seabol, Mike Mahoney and John Gall.

Because of significant injuries to Scott Rolen, Reggie Sanders, Larry Walker and Yadier Molina, the Cardinals' lineup card usually looked as if it had been filled out for a spring training game. But the team's ability to churn out wins with various player combinations became one of the major story lines of the 2005 season. New faces popped in and out of the lineup, and familiar ones appeared at unexpected positions or lineup spots. Play Luna—an infielder by trade—in right field? Sure. Bat Molina—a lost cause at the plate in April—cleanup at times? Why not. The 2004 offense was built largely on the big bang, but the '05 team squeezed out runs in any manner possible.

The clear MVPs of this unheralded group were Nunez and Taguchi. On the advice of scout Jim Leyland, the Cardinals invited Nunez to spring training. He played well enough to earn a roster spot, then thrived as a utility player. His value to the team became fully realized when Rolen first hurt his shoulder in May, and then again when Rolen went down for good in July. Nunez played nifty defense at third and displayed excellent bat control. He hit .375 in June and .354 in July.

Taguchi hit for a solid average and provided surprising pop and clutch hits. This from a guy who was mocked for constantly getting overmatched when he came to the Cardinals in 2002. Always fundamentally and defensively sound, Taguchi came through in just about every situation in which he was thrust.

Which, after all, is what the 2005 Cardinals were all about.

The First ...

Game: Cardinals 4, Braves 3, 12 innings (May 12, 1966).

Pitching victory: The Cardinals' Don Dennis (May 12).

Hit: A single by the Braves' Gary Geiger (May 12).

Run: The Cardinals' Jerry Buchek (May 12).

Double: Geiger (May 12).

Triple: The Cardinals' Mike Shannon (May 12).

Home run: The Braves' Felipe Alou (May 12).

Multihomer game: Alou, two home runs (May 12).

Grand slam: The Cardinals' Curt Flood vs. Cubs (May 25).

RBI: Shannon (May 12).

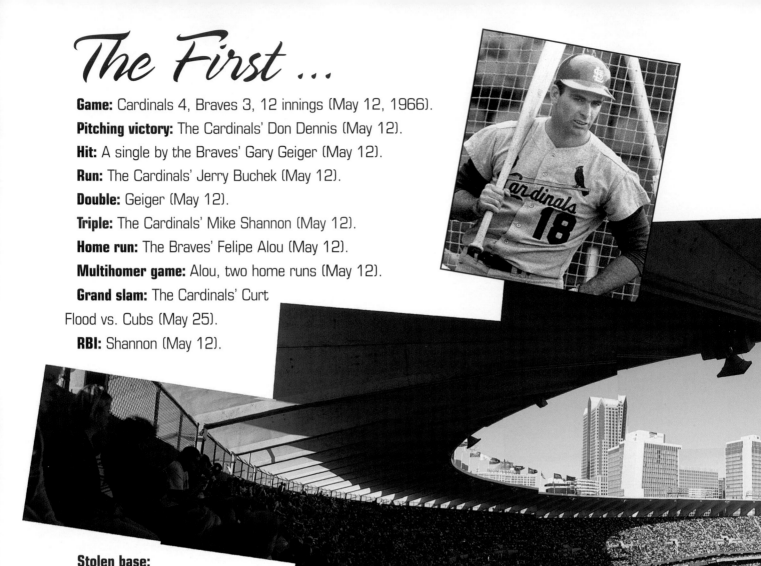

Stolen base: The Cardinals' Lou Brock (May 15).

Batter: Alou (May 12).

1-0 game: Dodgers 1, Cardinals 0 (June 1).

Extra-inning game: May 12.

Walk-off win: May 12 (Brock singled in the 12th to score Flood).

Triple play: By the Cardinals vs. Astros (May 8, 1977). Willie Crawford's line drive was caught by second baseman Mike Tyson, whose throw to shortstop Don Kessinger doubled up Enos Cabell at second. Kessinger's throw to first baseman Keith Hernandez caught Cesar Cedeno off the bag.

The Final ...

Game: Astros 5, Cardinals 1 (October 19, 2005, Game 6 of NLCS).

Pitching victory: The Astros' Roy Oswalt (October 19).

Hit: A single by the Cardinals' Mark Grudzielanek (October 19).

Run: The Astros' Craig Biggio (October 19).

Double: The Cardinals' Larry Walker (October 19).

Triple: The Astros' Adam Everett (October 13, 2005, Game 2 of NLCS).

Home run: The Astros' Jason Lane (October 19).

Multihomer game: Walker, two home runs, vs. Reds (October 1, 2005).

Grand slam: The Cardinals' Reggie Sanders vs. Padres (October 4, 2005, Game 1 of NLDS).

RBI: The Astros' Morgan Ensberg (October 19).

Stolen base: The Astros' Brad Ausmus (October 13).

Batter: The Cardinals' Yadier Molina (October 19).

1-0 game: Cardinals 1, Astros 0, 10 innings (April 23, 2005).

Extra-inning game: Cubs 8, Cardinals 4, 10 innings (July 24, 2005).

Walk-off win: Cardinals 5, Pirates 4 (September 13, 2005). David Eckstein singled in the ninth to score Hector Luna.

Triple play: By the Cardinals vs. Padres (May 5, 2005). Ramon Hernandez's line drive was caught by Albert Pujols, who stepped on first base for the second out and then threw to shortstop Eckstein, who tagged out Phil Nevin.

41

Top 5 games at Busch in 2005

1. August 7: Cardinals 5, Braves 3. Trailing 3-1 in the bottom of the ninth, the Cardinals strung together two-strike singles by Abraham Nunez, So Taguchi and Hector Luna. Following a popup, David Eckstein (above) jumped on a 1-0 pitch and pulled it down the left field line for a walk-off grand slam, the first by a Cardinal since Tommy Herr in 1987.

2. August 19: Cardinals 5, Giants 4. Down 4-0 with three outs remaining, the Cardinals got a double by John Mabry, a single by Taguchi and a home run by Yadier Molina. John Rodriguez and Nunez then singled around a sacrifice by Eckstein. With two outs, Jim Edmonds doubled into the right-center gap to score pinch runner Luna and Nunez, completing a five-run ninth-inning uprising.

3. April 23: Cardinals 1, Astros 0 (10 innings). An old-fashioned pitchers duel, with the Astros' Roger Clemens throwing seven shutout innings and the Cards' Mark Mulder pitching 10 scoreless frames. The Cardinals broke through in the bottom of the 10th, as Reggie Sanders scored on Larry Walker's hit to the warning track off Brad Lidge, a Cardinals nemesis from the 2004 NLCS. Clemens also was victimized by a Cardinals shutout on July 17, when he lost, 3-0, to Chris Carpenter, who threw a three-hitter in a game that took 1 hour, 59 minutes.

4. July 15: Cardinals 4, Astros 3 (13 innings). Lefties Mulder and Andy Pettitte of the Astros both were sharp. In the bottom of the eighth, catcher Einar Diaz broke a 1-1 tie with a homer. The Astros tied the game against Jason Isringhausen in the ninth and went ahead, 3-2, in the top of the 13th on a single by Mike Lamb off Ray King. In the bottom of the inning, Eckstein led off with a walk. Then, with one out, Albert Pujols hit a walk-off homer into the left field bullpen.

5. July 22: Cardinals 2, Cubs 1 (11 innings). Carpenter and Carlos Zambrano matched one-run gems over nine innings. In the top of the 10th, the Cubs loaded the bases against Isringhausen, but he got Aramis Ramirez to ground out to end the threat. Mabry tripled off the left field wall to lead off the bottom of the 11th. With one out, Eckstein laid down a suicide squeeze to score pinch runner Luna. Eckstein also had a game-winning squeeze in the ninth inning on July 6 in Arizona.

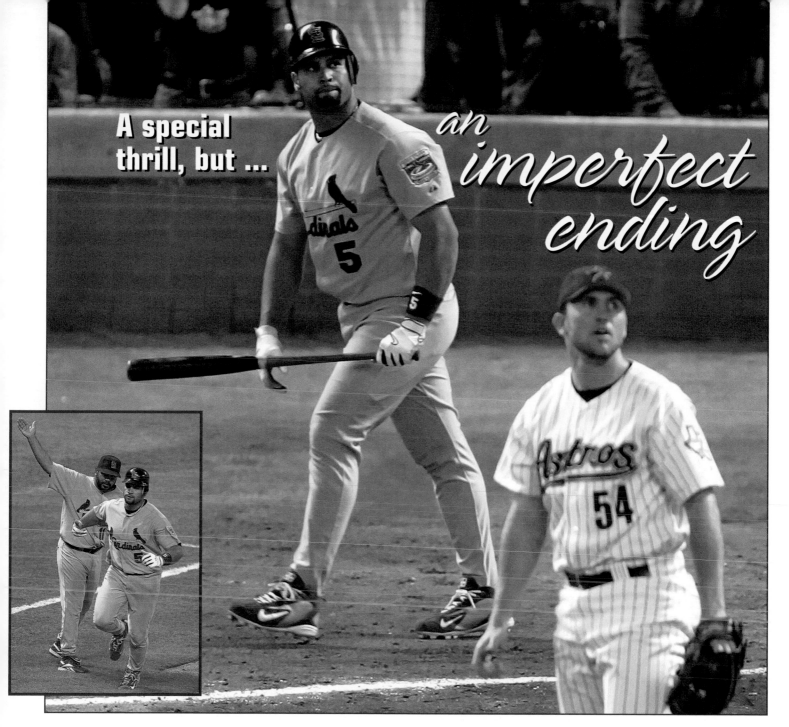

A special thrill, but ... *an imperfect ending*

The Cardinals, trailing 4-2, were one strike away from seeing their season end in Game 5 of the 2005 NLCS against the Astros. But David Eckstein singled, Jim Edmonds walked and **Albert Pujols** gave Cardinals fans a memory for a lifetime. Brad Lidge threw an 0-1 slider and Pujols launched a prodigious homer that wound up on the railroad tracks in the upper reaches of left field in Minute Maid Park. One swing made the sports world buzz. One swing gave the Cardinals a life.

Alas, it extended the season for only one game.

In Game 6, Roy Oswalt dominated the Cardinals just as he had in Game 2, and the Astros qualified for their first World Series by brushing aside the Cardinals. It was the last game ever at Busch Stadium, the ending

of a season that saw the Cardinals win 100 games and then the first four in the playoffs. But they lost four of their last five and ultimately were undone by an offense that scored 16 runs in six NLCS games.

That was a marked difference from the NLDS, in which St. Louis pounded its way past the Padres in a three-game sweep. In each game, the Cardinals built big early leads and then cruised behind strong pitching efforts by Chris Carpenter, Mark Mulder and Matt Morris. St. Louis rode the hot bat of Reggie Sanders, who hit a grand slam in the opener and drove in 10 runs in the three games.

At postseason's dawn, the Cardinals had dreams of closing Busch Stadium with a World Series championship. They had to settle for the Minute Maid miracle.

Where Mike Shannon's 1964 World Series
homer bounced off scoreboard

Where one-armed outfielder Pete
Gray made big-league debut for
Browns, April 17, 1945

Basepaths where Enos
Slaughter made his Mad Dash
to win seventh game of
1946 World Series

Landing point
for final-day,
ninth-inning grand slam by
Hank Greenberg that gave
Tigers 6-3 win over
Browns and 1945
A.L. pennant

MVP Ken Boyer led Cardinals to 1964
pennant; Bob Gibson secured World
Series championship with Game 7 win
over Yankees

Cardinals brought 10 pennants,
seven championships
to Sportsman's Park

Where Browns' Bob Cain
outdueled Indians star Bob
Feller 1-0 in double one-hitter,
April 23, 1952

STAN THE MAN MUSIAL:
Cardinals' three-time MVP,
seven-time batting champ
collected 3,630 career hits,
fourth all-time

Musial goes crazy:
five home runs,
nine RBIs in
doubleheader vs.
Giants,
May 2, 1954

Browns' Bobo Holloman fires no-hitter in
first major league start, May 6, 1953

Before there was Busch Stadium, there was ...

Sportsman's PARK

1892, 1920-1966

Point where Max West's All-Star Game-deciding home run landed in 1940

Point where one of Babe Ruth's three Game 4 home runs cleared bleachers in 1926 World Series, breaking auto dealer's window across Grand Avenue

A screen ran from the top of the fence to the roof of the right field pavilion

SCHICK INJECTOR RAZOR
Fast Becoming America's Most Popular Razor

Great defensive shortstop Marty Marion wins 1944 MVP, Cardinals defeat Browns in World Series—the only all-St. Louis fall classic

Chet Laabs homers twice, Browns beat Yankees 5-2 and win only A.L. pennant, Oct. 1, 1944

A long line of great Cardinals second basemen: Rogers Hornsby, Frank Frisch, Red Schoendienst, Julian Javier

Browns first baseman George Sisler (right) batted .420 and compiled 41-game hitting streak in 1922; six-time Cardinals batting champ Rogers Hornsby hit .424 in 1924

DIZZY DEAN: Cardinals clinched pennant on final day of 1934 season—Dean won No. 30 that afternoon, beating Reds, 9-0

Dean brothers, Dizzy and Paul, combined for 49 wins in 1934

Ty Cobb, Tigers' 38-year-old player-manager, hits 3 homers, double, 2 singles and drives in 5 runs in 14-8 win over Browns, May 5, 1925

Batter's box where Eddie Gaedel, Bill Veeck's midget, drew walk in surprise appearance vs. Tigers, Aug. 19, 1951

Fans manage Browns in another Veeck promotional stunt, Aug. 24, 1951

St. Louis had a National League team in 1876, the league's first season, and again in 1877. After dropping out of the N.L., the city resurfaced as a league member in 1885 and 1886, only to see its team disband once more.

It was in 1892 that the Cardinals' lineage began. That year, four teams from the American Association (a major league from 1882 through 1891) joined the National League. One of those franchises was owner Chris Von der Ahe's St. Louis Browns, who eventually were renamed the Perfectos and then the Cardinals.

That 1892 N.L. team—vastly different in personnel from the club that competed the year before in

the Association—played its first season at Grand Avenue and Dodier Street, where numerous structures called Sportsman's Park, with different configurations, would exist over the years. From 1893 through June 1920, the club played at Robison Field (Natural Bridge and Vandeventer avenues).

With the American League's St. Louis Browns owning Sportsman's Park until 1953—they first played at Grand and Dodier in 1902—and the Cardinals serving as tenants beginning in July 1920, Sportsman's played host to major league baseball through May 8, 1966. In early 1953, when Anheuser-Busch Inc. purchased the Cardinals and the ballpark, the facility was

renamed Busch Stadium. (After the '53 season, the Browns moved to Baltimore.)

When the Cardinals moved into new Busch Memorial Stadium in 1966, August A. Busch Jr. donated the Sportsman's site to the Herbert Hoover Boys and Girls Club.

First game at Grand and Dodier site: April 12, 1892. The Cardinals (Browns at the time) lost to Chicago, 14-10.

Final game: May 8, 1966. The Cardinals lost to the Giants, 10-5.

Site of 10 World Series (1926, '28, '30, '31, '34, '42, '43, '44, '46, and '64).

Site of 3 All-Star Games (1940, '48 and '57).

Hall of Fame LEGENDS

Career stats:
.358 batting average
301 home runs
1,584 RBIs

1942

HORNSBY
Rogers

POSITION 2nd base   **CARDINALS SEASONS 1915-26, 1933**

When Cardinals manager Miller Huggins told a 135-pound youngster named Rogers Hornsby that he was not big enough for the major leagues, it meant the infielder was being farmed out—but not in the manner known nowadays.

Hornsby spent the winter of 1915-16 working on his uncle's farm, and he added 25 pounds of muscle to his frame. When he reported to spring training in 1916 at the ripe old age of 19, he looked like a different player.

Hornsby won a job with the Cardinals and stayed with the club through the 1926 season, becoming one of the most-feared hitters in the game. He won the Triple Crown twice, captured six consecutive batting titles, topped the .400 mark three times in four years and was the manager/second baseman for the Cardinals' first World Series champion, the '26 team. He would say years later that despite all of his offensive exploits, his greatest baseball thrill was tagging out Babe Ruth to end the '26 Series. Ruth was attempting to steal second base, but catcher Bob O'Farrell threw him out.

Never one to shy away from a confrontation, Hornsby was often at odds with Cardinals owner Sam Breadon. But news after the '26 season that Hornsby had been traded to the Giants for Frankie Frisch still left St. Louis fans shaken.

Highlights: Considered the greatest righthanded hitter of all time ... His .424 average in 1924 was the majors' best in the 20th century ... Had 250 hits in 1922 after collecting 235 the year before ... In one five-year span, he hit .402 ... Also played for Giants, Braves, Cubs and Browns.

Career stats:
.316 batting average
2,880 hits
419 stolen bases

Trading one of the game's greatest players is never a popular move. Cardinals owner Sam Breadon was heavily criticized—and then some—after dealing second baseman/manager Rogers Hornsby to the New York Giants in December 1926—10 weeks after the Cards had won their first World Series championship. St. Louis got second baseman Frankie Frisch and so-so pitcher Jimmy Ring for Hornsby, who had batted .400-plus three times for the Cardinals.

When Frisch had a bad day defensively in his first exhibition game in a Cardinals uniform, the attacks only intensified. Frisch proceeded to calm St. Louis fans' fears with a spectacular 1927 season, and he wound up playing 11 years in St. Louis—a stint during which he managed the team in its Gas House Gang era.

Highly educated and possessing a multitude of interests besides baseball, Frisch was a fiery competitor. He was frequently at odds with more relaxed players—some of whom didn't always take the game as seriously as Frisch, a man who had no time for those who committed mental mistakes, questioned his authority or failed to give 100 percent.

As it turned out, Hornsby made the Hall of Fame in 1942. Frisch was enshrined in 1947, after hitting above .325 eight times in his 19-year major league career, winning three National League stolen base titles and managing the 1934 Cardinals to a World Series crown.

It wasn't such a bad trade after all, Mr. Breadon.

Highlights: N.L. MVP in 1931, when he batted .311 with 82 RBIs and a league-high 28 steals ... Hit the first N.L. home run in All-Star Game history, connecting in the inaugural game in 1933 ... Managed the Cardinals from 1933 to 1938, guiding the Gas House Gang to the 1934 World Series title.

1947

Dizzy

POSITION Pitcher   **UNIFORM NO 17**   **CARDINALS SEASONS 1930, 1932-37**

Never has a player had a more appropriate nickname than Jay Hanna Dean, the man known as "Dizzy."

When he was pitching in the minor leagues in St. Joseph, Mo., Dean had rooms booked at three hotels so he could stay wherever it was most convenient. In Philadelphia, he and a few Cardinals teammates donned overalls and acted like construction workers as they interrupted a banquet. And, the story goes, he once walked a hitter with two out in the ninth inning so he could pitch to Bill Terry. Dizzy walked in from the mound and told Terry he had promised some hospitalized kids he would strike out Terry that day. He did, too.

Dean always said it wasn't bragging if you could back up your words. After he threw a three-hit shutout at Brooklyn in the first game of a doubleheader in 1934, he watched brother Paul throw a no-hitter in the nightcap. Diz said that if he had known Paul was going to pitch a no-hitter, he would have hurled one, too.

By the time he was 25 years old, Dean had won 121 games in the majors, led the National League in strikeouts four times and twice topped the league in wins. In '34 he went 30-7. He remains the last National Leaguer to win 30 games in one season.

After breaking a toe in the 1937 All-Star Game, Dean altered his pitching motion and suffered an arm injury. He never won a game after age 29. But he had made his mark, with his swagger and his arm. His career winning percentage: .644.

Career stats:

    victories

    winning pct.

    ERA

    shutouts

Highlights: N.L.
MVP in 1934, when
he went 30-7 with a
2.66 ERA and 195
strikeouts ... **Won 20 or
more games in four
consecutive seasons ...**
Bragged about his hitting—had
29 hits in '34 and 30 in 1935.

1953

1968

Highlights: Nicknamed "Ducky" for the way he walked ... Won the N.L. Triple Crown in 1937, hitting .374 with 31 home runs and 154 RBIs. Also named N.L. MVP that season ... Played in 10 All-Star Games, six as a Cardinal ... Led the league in RBIs three consecutive years.

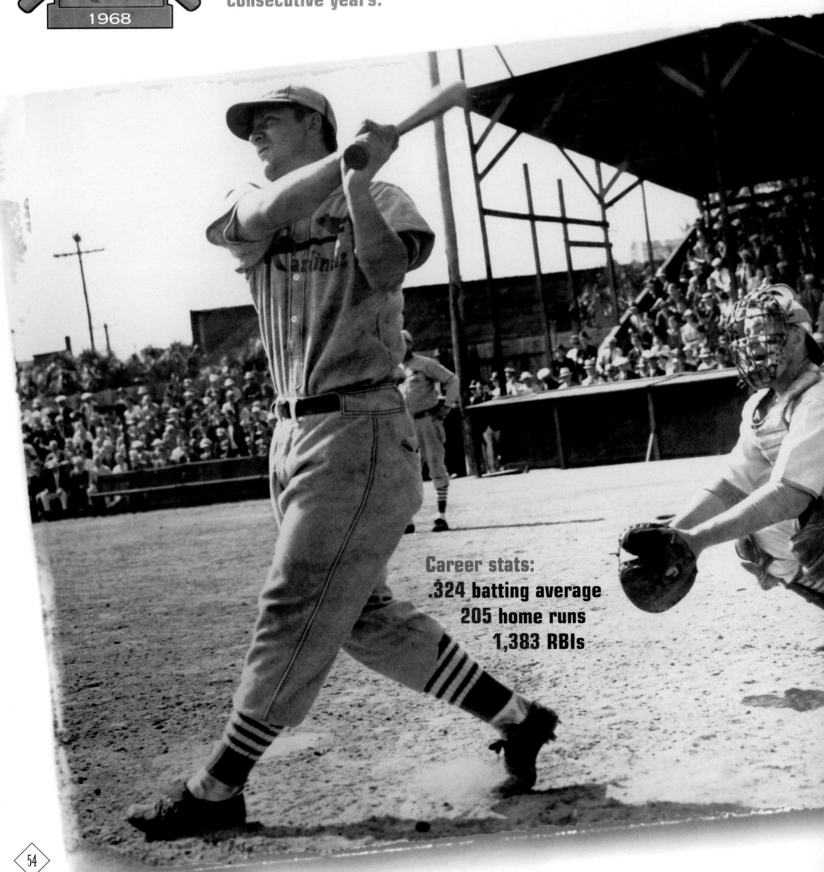

Career stats:
.324 batting average
205 home runs
1,383 RBIs

MEDWICK Joe

Joe Medwick was known primarily for two things during his Cardinals career—his success as a notorious bad-ball hitter and his penchant for never backing down from a fight, even if it meant taking on one or more of his teammates.

After Dizzy Dean and brother Paul once confronted Medwick in the dugout after he misplayed a fly ball into three runs for the opposition, Medwick soon responded with a grand slam. He then spat a mouthful of water at Dizzy's feet and followed with a "Let's see if you can keep that lead" challenge.

Medwick turned down a scholarship to play football at Notre Dame, so there was no questioning his toughness. It was his hard slide into Tigers third baseman Marv Owen that threatened to turn Game 7 of the 1934 World Series into a riot. With the Cardinals on the way to a blowout victory, commissioner Kenesaw Mountain Landis quieted an angry Detroit crowd by ordering Medwick's removal from the game in the sixth inning.

The man known as "Ducky" was an RBI machine for the Cardinals from 1933 through 1939, driving in 861 runs over those seven seasons. He won the Triple Crown in 1937 and remains the last National Leaguer to accomplish that feat.

A Cardinal since 1932, Medwick was traded to the Dodgers in 1940 and also played for the Giants and Braves. Fittingly, he concluded his stellar major league career—he batted .324 over 17 seasons—with the Cardinals, playing sparingly for his old team in 1947 and 1948.

MUSIAL
Stan

Career stats:
.331 batting
average
475 home runs
1,951 RBIs
3,630 hits

1969

Signed to a professional baseball contract out of the mining hills of Pennsylvania when he was only 17 years old, Stan Musial hardly appeared destined to become the greatest player in Cardinals history.

Musial was signed as a pitcher and started out making $65 a month. By his third season in the minors, 1940, he was still in the low reaches of St. Louis' farm system, playing for Daytona Beach of the Class D Florida State League.

In what appeared to be a break-through year, though, Musial compiled an 18-5 record in 28 mound appearances in '40 and, showing a good bat, also saw extensive duty in the outfield. But, late in the season, he suffered a setback: Attempting to make a shoe-string catch, he fell heavily on his left (pitching) shoulder. A knot developed, and Musial wondered if his baseball career was over.

Daytona Beach manager Dickie Kerr, the former White Sox pitcher, persuaded Musial not to quit the game. In the spring of 1941,

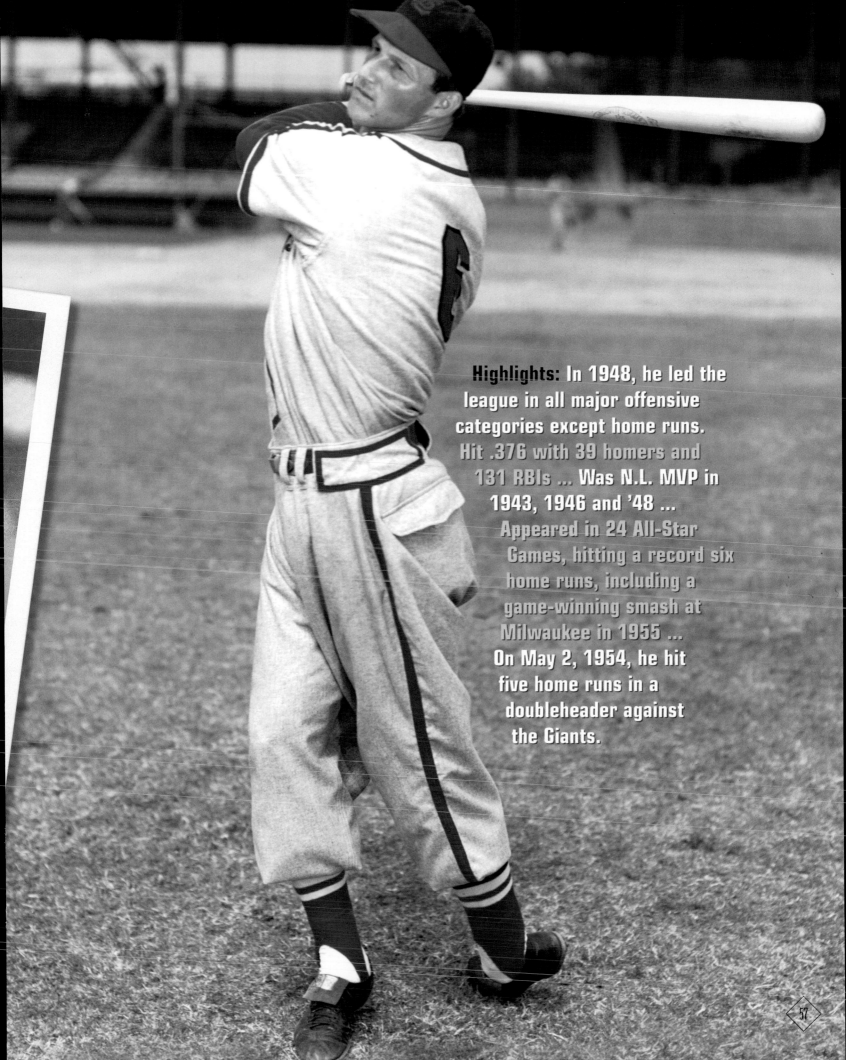

Highlights: In 1948, he led the league in all major offensive categories except home runs. Hit .376 with 39 homers and 131 RBIs ... Was N.L. MVP in 1943, 1946 and '48 ... Appeared in 24 All-Star Games, hitting a record six home runs, including a game-winning smash at Milwaukee in 1955 ... On May 2, 1954, he hit five home runs in a doubleheader against the Giants.

57

Cardinals executive Branch Rickey and his lieutenant, Burt Shotton, talked manager Ollie Vanek into taking Musial on his roster as an outfielder for the Cards' Class C team in Springfield, Mo.

Success followed immediately. Musial began hitting the ball for average and power, and he rose from Springfield to Rochester of the International League as the season wore on. By the end of September, he found himself in the major leagues, where he batted .426 for the Cardinals in 12 games.

Excluding one year in military service, Musial proceeded to hit line drives for the next 21 seasons. Along the way, he won seven National League batting titles.

By the time he retired in 1963, after collecting career hit No. 3,630 in his last at-bat and finishing with a .331 lifetime batting average, Musial was recognized as one of game's all-time elite players. His nickname, "Stan the Man," had come by way of Brooklyn, where fans moaned every time they saw "that man" coming to the plate. Musial hit well everywhere, but he found cozy Ebbets Field particularly inviting.

Musial won three N.L. Most Valuable Player awards, captured his first batting title in 1943 at age 22 and his last in 1957, when he was 36. He led the N.L. in doubles eight times, was tops in triples five times and was No. 1 in runs scored five times. Even though he was never considered a top-of-the-line home run hitter, he finished just 25 homers shy of the coveted 500 mark.

He missed the Triple Crown by only one home run in 1948 (a year in which he batted .376, hit 39 homers and drove in 131 runs). Never one to complain about such matters, Musial exhibited a grace and friendliness throughout his career that endeared him more to teammates and fans than his baseball skill did—and that is saying a lot. After all, with a bat in his hand, the Cardinals' Stan Musial was truly "The Man."

When Jesse Haines began losing some of the zip on his fastball, he knew he had to come up with another pitch if he wanted to stay in the major leagues.

That pitch was a knuckleball, taught to him by Philadelphia A's righthander Ed Rommel. It was different than the knuckleball of the modern era, because the ball actually was gripped with the knuckles, not the fingertips. The pitch acted more like a spitball and didn't flutter.

Haines was the starting pitcher in Game 7 of the 1926 World Series, and he limited the Yankees to two runs through 6⅔ innings before a sore finger (the result of his knuckleball grip rubbing away some skin) and a mounting New York threat forced him out of the game. Grover Cleveland Alexander came on in relief and struck out Tony Lazzeri with the bases loaded. Six outs later, the Cardinals were World Series champions for the first time.

One of Haines' most memorable games came in a losing effort against Alexander and the Cubs in Jesse's rookie season, 1920. He and Alexander both went the distance in a 17-inning game that Chicago won, 3-2. Haines didn't allow a hit from the seventh inning through the 16th.

In 1924, Haines pitched the first no-hitter in Cardinals history, shutting down the Boston Braves, 5-0, at Sportsman's Park.

Haines spent 18 years with the Cardinals, the longest pitching tenure in club history, and he won 210 games, second on the Cards' all-time list to Bob Gibson's 251.

1970

Career stats:
victories
winning pct.
ERA

Highlights: Won 20 games three times, with a high of 24 victories in 1927, a season in which he pitched 25 complete games ... Threw the first no-hitter in Cardinals history on July 17, 1924 ... Pitched 554 of his 555 major league games for the Cards. Made one appearance for the Reds at the outset of his career.

) 19½ PIX 5 5/16" NEWS   R-67½

HAFEY

Chick

Chick Hafey's career statistics are impressive by any yardstick. But when you consider that Hafey performed at a Hall of Fame level despite serious vision problems, his accomplishments are downright amazing.

Branch Rickey, one of the best judges of talent in the game's history, believed that Hafey—if blessed with normal eyesight and good health—might have become the best righthanded hitter baseball had ever known.

Beaned several times during the 1926 season (when he was 23 years old), Hafey began wearing glasses on a doctor's recommendation. He had so much trouble with his eyes that he had three pair of glasses, with different prescriptions, and the outfielder selected his eyewear depending on how his vision was on a particular day. His sight also was affected by a serious sinus condition.

Teammates said that on bad days, Hafey had trouble making out the red "Exit" sign on a railroad car.

Despite his physical problems, Hafey won the National League batting title in 1931, edging the Giants' Bill Terry and Cardinals teammate Jim Bottomley, and in the process he led the Cardinals to their fourth pennant in six years.

Amid a contract dispute, Hafey, a .326 hitter over eight seasons with St. Louis, was traded to the Reds in April 1932. Poor vision continued to hamper him, and by 1937—at age 34—he was playing his final season in the majors.

Highlights: Won the N.L. batting title in 1931 in one of the tightest races ever in the majors. Hafey finished at .3489, the Giants' Bill Terry at .3486 and Cards teammate Jim Bottomley at .3482 ... Hit .336 or higher four straight seasons.

1971

Career stats:
.317 batting average
164 home runs
833 RBIs

1974

Career stats:
.310 batting average
219 home runs
2,313 hits
1,422 RBIs

Highlights: Known as "Sunny Jim" ... Greatest game came on September 16, 1924, at Ebbets Field in Brooklyn, when he drove in 12 runs and went 6-for-6 ... Named N.L. MVP in 1928, a year in which he hit 31 home runs, batted .325 and drove in 136 runs ... Played for the St. Louis Browns in 1936 and 1937, becoming manager midway through the '37 season when the Browns fired Rogers Hornsby.

It was the promise and the eventual success of such young players as Jim Bottomley that convinced Branch Rickey to develop players through a network of minor league affiliates.

At age 19, Bottomley was playing semipro ball in Illinois and working as a blacksmith apprentice when he was discovered and signed by a Cardinals scout. Three years later, in 1922, he was playing first base in the major leagues.

Rickey figured that by controlling and grooming his own players from the days they entered the pro ranks, he would have the edge on teams that signed and purchased players merely as opportunities arose. And by the time Bottomley (just the kind of young player Rickey envisioned) was in his third full season in the majors, Rickey had an eight-team farm system in place.

As for the career of the man known as "Sunny" because of his easygoing disposition, there was a lot to smile about during Bottomley's 11 seasons with the Cardinals. He drove in 111 or more runs for six consecutive years and won the National League's MVP award in 1928. He also played on the Cardinals' first World Series championship team and their first four pennant-winning clubs.

Other players smiled when they were around Bottomley—not just because of his lusty hitting, but also because of his naivete. Early in his career, he noticed a long, slender bat in the dugout rack. Turning to a veteran pitcher, he asked, "Pardon me, sir, but who is this Mr. Fungo?"

The biggest smile on Bottomley's face came on September 16, 1924, when he established a major league record by driving in 12 runs in one game (a mark tied 69 years later by another Cardinals player, Mark Whiten). Bottomley's big day—he went 6-for-6 against Brooklyn at Ebbets Field—featured a grand slam and a two-run homer. He also had a run-scoring double and three singles that knocked in five runs.

Two leg injuries almost ended Johnny Mize's major league career before it began. Mize "retired" in 1935, his sixth minor league season, but the parent Cardinals weren't convinced he should give up the game. Cards executives summoned Mize to St. Louis for a medical examination.

Dr. Robert F. Hyland, the team physician, diagnosed the injury as bone spurs and performed an operation. Because he couldn't play every day in 1936 until fully recovered from surgery, Mize remained in St. Louis with the thought that he could see occasional duty as a Cardinals pinch hitter.

When his legs healed, Mize settled in as the Cards' first baseman and had six stellar seasons ('36 through 1941) with St. Louis. He drove in 653 runs and captured a National League batting title in that span. His 43 home runs in 1940 led the majors and stood as the Cardinals' single-season record until the mark was broken by Mark McGwire in 1998.

Mize, who was traded to the New York Giants in December 1941 and had a 51-homer season for the Giants six years later, earned the nickname "Big Cat" for his defensive abilities at first base, but he is remembered more for his offensive exploits. In Cardinals history, only three players have led the league at least once in batting average, doubles, triples and home runs—Rogers Hornsby, Joe Medwick and Mize.

Although he never played on a pennant-winner with the Cardinals, Mize wound up his career by appearing in five consecutive World Series with the Yankees.

Career stats:
.312 batting average
359 home runs
1,337 RBIs

Highlights: The Big Cat played in 10 All-Star Games, four as a Cardinal ... Topped the league in homers four times—twice as a Cardinal, twice as a Giant ... Batted an N.L.-leading .349 for St. Louis in 1939 and hit .364 for the Cards in 1937.

MVP

Johnny

POSITION 1st base   **UNIFORM NO** 10   **CARDINALS SEASONS** 1936-41

1981

Highlights: His hallmark season was 1968, when he went 22-9 with 13 shutouts and a 1.12 ERA (the lowest figure in major league history) ... Five-time 20-game winner ... Won Cy Young Award in 1968 and 1970 and N.L. MVP honor in '68 ... Had 28 complete games in '68 and '69.

Career stats:
251 victories
2.91 ERA
3,117 strikeouts
56 shutouts

GIBSON

Bob

Many longtime baseball observers agree that if there was one game they absolutely had to win, the pitcher they would want on the mound is Bob Gibson.

Gibson didn't talk to opponents. He barely talked to his St. Louis teammates on the days he was pitching, and he rarely smiled. Gibson's competitiveness was part of what made him so successful. He once hit a batter in a spring-training game because the player had attempted a bunt. He dusted off former teammates. He glowered.

Gibson was at his fiercest competitive level in the biggest games. In nine career World Series starts, he fashioned a composite 1.89 ERA. In his spectacular 1968 season, a year in which he posted an unfathomable 1.12 ERA and threw 13 shutouts, Gibson had one stretch in which he allowed only two runs in 95 innings. When a line drive off the bat of Roberto Clemente broke his right leg in July 1967, Gibson faced three more batters before falling to the ground. He knew he was hurting, but he didn't know he had suffered a fracture.

It was partly because of Gibson's performance in '68 that baseball officials decided to lower the mound from 15 inches to 10 inches in an effort to inject more offense into the game. The move worked—except, of course, when Gibson was pitching.

1981

SLAUGHTER

Enos

POSITION Outfield   **UNIFORM NO 9**   **CARDINALS SEASONS** 1938-42, 1946-53

His career is remembered primarily because of one play—the first-to-home "mad dash" in Game 7 that won the 1946 World Series for the Cardinals over the Boston Red Sox. But Enos Slaughter's tenure with the Cardinals was, in fact, multi-faceted.

The fiercely competitive Slaughter was a mainstay in the Cardinals' outfield for 13 seasons. He inspired countless youngsters to play the game the proper way—by hustling all of the time, advice he received as a minor leaguer and never forgot. His all-out style made him a quintessential St. Louis Cardinal, and he wore the uniform proudly.

Slaughter, who missed three prime years because of military service, hit .300 or higher in eight of 13 seasons with St. Louis. He drove in 100-plus runs three times and scored 100 runs three times. In 1946, he had 18 home runs and 130 RBIs; in 1949, he batted .336. During the 1940s, when he teamed with Stan Musial and Terry Moore, the Cardinals' outfield was considered one of the greatest of all time.

If his 1946 sprint to home plate was the highlight of his Cardinals career, the darkest day for Slaughter came in April 1954, when he was traded to the Yankees. No injury he had ever suffered hurt quite as much.

Career stats:
.300 batting average
2,383 hits
1,304 RBIs

1985

Highlights: Played in 10 All-Star Games as a Cardinal and hit .381 ... In 1949, he batted .336 with 96 RBIs ... Topped 100-RBI mark three times and had a league-leading 130 RBIs in 1946 ... Had 10 or more triples in a season seven times ... Traded to the Yankees in 1954. Played in more World Series as a Yankee (three) than as a Cardinal (two).

To most people, the distance between first base and second base is 90 feet. To Lou Brock, it was 13 steps.

A math major in college, Brock viewed the art of basestealing differently than most. It was no surprise, of course, when Brock set out to steal; whenever he reached first base at Busch Stadium, chants of "Lou, Lou, Lou" echoed throughout the ballpark. He viewed the inner game between himself and the pitcher and catcher as psychological warfare. Everyone knew he was going to go, but only Brock knew when—and exactly how many steps the journey would take.

Much of the reason for Brock's success, both as a hitter and a basestealer, was his attitude. He wasn't afraid to fail—in fact, Brock was driven to be successful, and it was never more apparent starting in June 1964 when St. Louis acquired the outfielder from the Cubs in a trade that some "experts" at the time believed favored the Chicago club. Once he put on a Cardinals uniform, Brock played like a man possessed. He sparked the Cards to the '64 pennant, hitting .348 and stealing 33 bases in 103 games.

The big name who went the other way in the deal, former 20-game winner Ernie Broglio, won only seven games in the rest of his career. Brock, who later had a 118-steal season and finished his career with 938 stolen bases and 3,023 hits, won a lot more—the hearts of every Cardinals fan.

Highlights: Set major league season (118) and career (938) stolen-base records. Both marks have been shattered by Rickey Henderson ... Helped the Cardinals to the 1967 World Series title with a .414 average, seven stolen bases and eight runs scored ... In the '68 Series, he hit .464 with another seven steals ... His career average in Series play: .391 ... 3,000th hit came off the Cubs' Dennis Lamp on August 13, 1979.

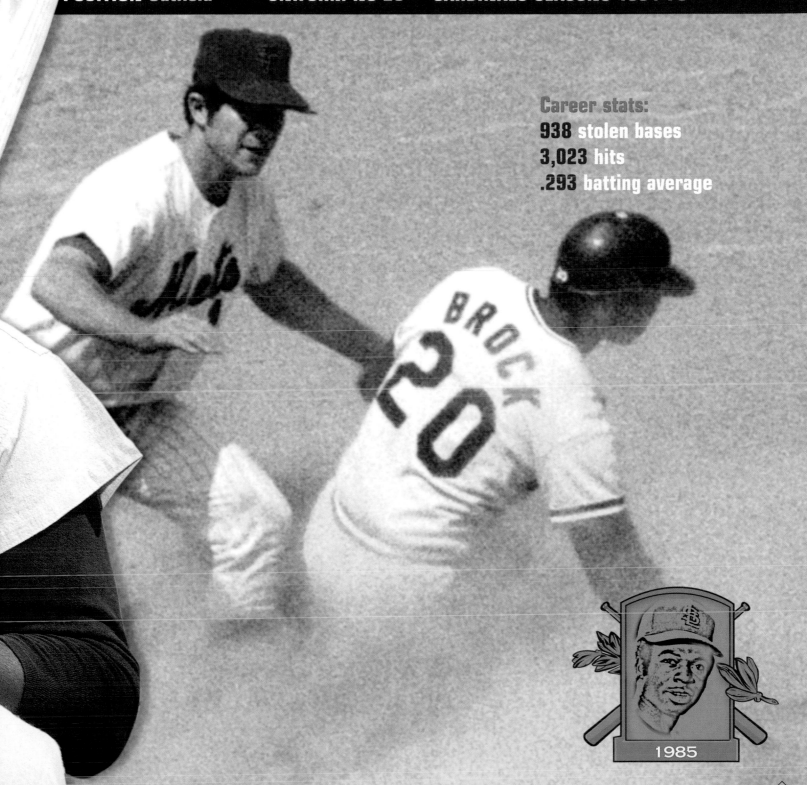

BROCK
Lou

POSITION Outfield　　UNIFORM NO 20　　CARDINALS SEASONS 1964-79

Career stats:
938 stolen bases
3,023 hits
.293 batting average

1985

SCHOENDIENST *Red*

Highlights: Led National League second basemen in fielding percentage seven times (four years as a Cardinal), still an N.L. record ... Played in eight All-Star Games as a Cardinal—won the 1950 game with a 14th-inning homer at Comiskey Park ... Not a power hitter but had 79-RBI seasons for St. Louis in 1953 and 1954.

Career stats:

.289 batting average

2,449 hits

.982 fielding pct.

1989

One of the least-appreciated persons in Cardinals history has to be the driver of the dairy truck who in the early 1940s picked up a red-haired boy in Illinois, a youngster who was hitchhiking to St. Louis to attend a tryout camp.

That boy, Albert "Red" Schoendienst, spent the night sleeping on a park bench outside the St. Louis train station before going out and impressing Cardinals executive Branch Rickey. The kid was signed to a minor league contract.

Rickey marveled at Schoendienst's natural ability, but he didn't know that the prospect would have been even better had it not been for an eye injury. When he was building fences a few years earlier, Schoendienst was struck in the eye by a ricocheting nail. Doctors at first feared they would have to remove the eye, but Schoendienst begged them not to take it, saying he was

going to be a baseball player.

The fact he worked so hard with eye exercises to overcome the injury was a testament to Schoendienst's work ethic, which he learned as young boy.

Red spent two-plus seasons in the minors, then went on to a 19-year major league career that featured 15 seasons with the Cardinals. The ever-dependable second baseman challenged for the National League batting title in 1953, batting .342. Three years earlier, he won the All-Star Game for the N.L. with a 14th-inning home run.

Named Cardinals manager in 1965, Schoendienst expected the same effort from his players that he had put forth. He guided the Cards for 12 seasons (along with two interim assignments), the longest managerial tenure in franchise history. In 1967, he directed St. Louis to the World Series championship.

After listening to Cardinals games for years, a young Harry Caray thought he could do a better job than the broadcasters on hand—so he asked radio station KMOX for a tryout. Caray got the audition, but he didn't get the position. He was terrible.

Caray, who grew up in the St. Louis area, finally earned a chance to do the games on a smaller station. And, after Cardinals owner Sam Breadon decided to have only one station carry the broadcasts in 1947, Caray was hired as the lead broadcaster. He wound up calling Cards game from 1945 through 1969.

The Cardinals had no bigger fan than Caray, and no one did a better job of selling the team. Because of the team's far-flung radio network (which featured smaller stations throughout the Midwest and South), Caray was the main source of information about the club for countless fans. He got emotionally involved on each play, too, saying he wanted his broadcasts to sound as if they were being called by a fan. And that's exactly how Caray's play-by-play came across.

When the Cardinals began their late-season surge for the pennant in 1964, Caray developed a jingle—"the Cardinals are coming, tra la la la." The refrain only increased his popularity, which by any standard was considerable.

1989

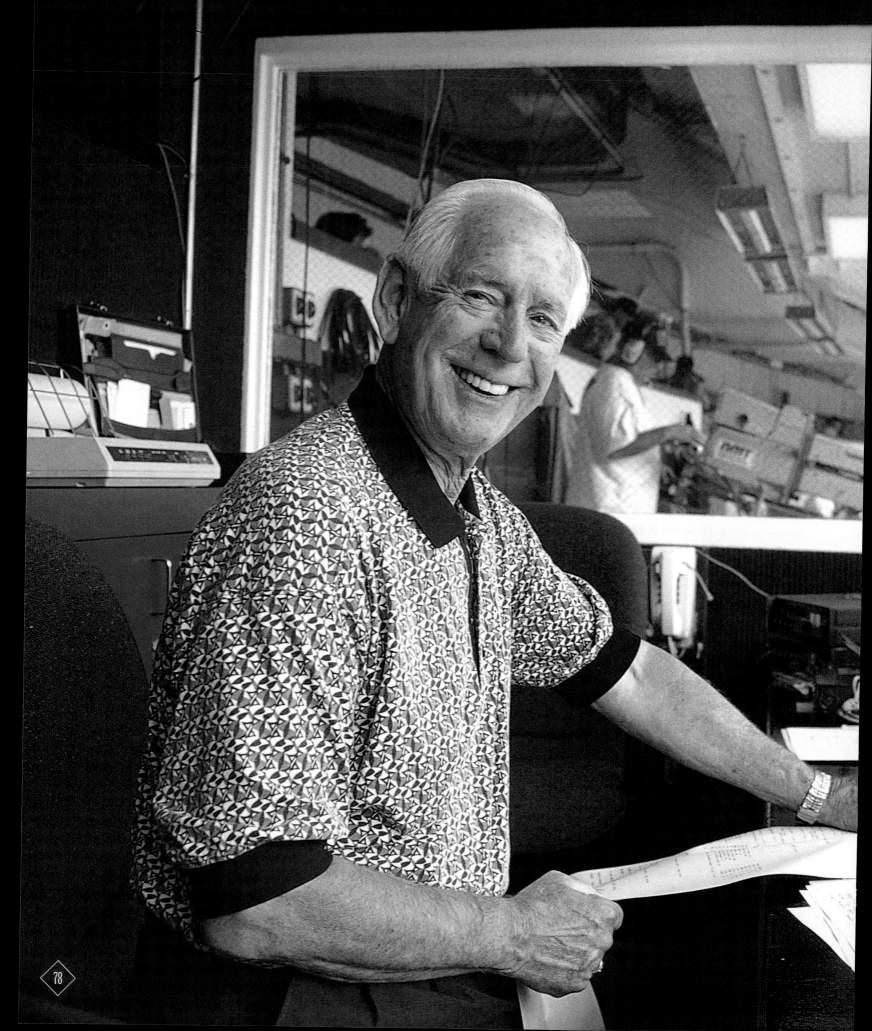

CARDINALS SEASONS 1954-59, 1961-01

St. Louis has had more than its share of popular and gifted baseball broadcasters, beginning with France Laux and continuing with Dizzy Dean, Harry Caray and Joe Garagiola. Yet the list will always be topped by Jack Buck.

Buck joined the Cardinals' radio team in 1954 and, with the exception of 1960, served as Caray's sidekick through the 1969 season. He moved into the No. 1 job in 1970 and remained there until his death in 2002.

Cardinals fans' recollections of the team's great moments over the last three decades are always linked to where the fans were and what they were doing when Buck made his memorable calls. Highlights included Bob Gibson's no-hitter; Lou Brock's record-breaking steals; Bruce Sutter's World Series-ending strikeout; Ozzie Smith and Jack Clark's postseason homers; and Mark McGwire's pursuit of Roger Maris' home run record.

1987

It was not unusual for fans to turn down the sound on their television sets so they could watch the game but listen to Buck's broadcast on radio. He had the ability to entertain, as well as inform, and to do it in his unique style.

Perhaps the biggest secret to his success was that he took the game—but not himself—seriously. Buck considered himself fortunate to be a baseball broadcaster, always remembering that the fans, ultimately, were his real bosses.

SMITH

Ozzie

POSITION Shortstop   **UNIFORM NO 1**   **CARDINALS SEASON 1982-96**

Ozz-ie, Ozz-ie, Ozz-ie.
Many things come to mind when Cardinals fans reflect on the glorious 1980s. Jack Clark rocketing balls to distant places. Willie McGee looking bad on one pitch, lacing the next into the gap. Vince Coleman stealing second—then third. John Tudor painting the corners. Fifty-thousand fans yelling *"Charge!"* during a rally. Nothing, however, was more identifiable than the chant showering down from all over Busch Stadium, the one directed at that wizard of a shortstop: *Ozz-ie, Ozz-ie, Ozz-ie.*

Ozzie Smith, perhaps the greatest defensive player in history, was the foundation for a team built on defense, speed and pitching. He could make every play: ranging deep behind second, short-hopping a high bouncer, diving into the hole and then popping off the turf like a Super Ball banging off a sidewalk, leaping over a baserunner while completing a double-play relay. Or, fans might best remember Smith—back to the infield—racing out and then diving to snare a blooper while also avoiding his own left fielder.

Acquired from the Padres for malcontent shortstop Garry Templeton before the 1982 season, Smith came to St. Louis with a great-glove, no-hit label. Half of that tag held up over time. Smith

2002

Highlights:

Hall of Fame Class 2002 ...
13-time Gold Glove winner ...
Led the league eight times in
fielding percentage, seven
times as a Cardinal ...
MVP runner-up in 1987 ...
Played in 14 All-Star Games.

Career stats:

.978 fielding pct.
2,460 hits
580 stolen bases

became a respected hitter, displaying excellent bat control while amassing nearly 2,500 career hits. His best season came in 1987, when he posted career highs with a .303 average, 104 runs and 75 RBIs. And the switch-hitting Smith was a key part of the team's go-go offense, averaging 37 steals from 1983 through '92.

Smith's most memorable moment was a game-winning homer against the Dodgers in the bottom of the ninth of Game 5 of the 1985 NLCS. It came off the Dodgers' Tom Niedenfuer, on a 1-2 pitch, the ball just clearing the right field wall. It was the first home run that Smith had hit lefthanded (in more than 3,000 at-

bats) in the major leagues. The improbability of it was underscored when Jack Buck screamed over the airwaves, "Go crazy, folks! Go crazy!" That call, perhaps the most famous in Buck's illustrious career, still rings clear in any Cardinals fan's head.

Smith, the player, had a style; he had *charisma*. Whether he was flashing a Hollywood smile, doing a backflip as he took his position for a really big game or tossing a ball behind his back to Tommy Herr for a forceout at second, Smith loved to put on a show. The question: Did he have more fun playing, or did we have more fun watching?

FIELDING PERCENTAGE

.978

A wizard with the glove, Ozzie Smith arrived with the reputation as a poor offensive player but made himself into a good hitter.

CHAMPIONS

1926
World Series Champions

Talk about having to win the pennant the hard way. After the Cardinals defeated the Pirates on September 1, 1926, they held a one-game lead over the Reds in the National League race. They also had just completed their home schedule.

Because of a scheduling quirk, the Cardinals had to play their final 24 regular-season games on the road—with a visit to each of their seven league rivals. The schedule certainly not in their favor, the Cards nevertheless played well enough on the road—they went 13-11—to claim the first pennant in franchise history. St. Louis finished two games ahead of Cincinnati.

The results might have been different if not for two front-office moves. On June 14, general manager Branch Rickey obtained outfielder Billy Southworth in a trade with the Giants. Southworth became the Cardinals' regular right fielder—and a solid contributor.

On June 22, Cardinals owner Sam Breadon saw that the Cubs had placed veteran pitcher Grover Cleveland Alexander on waivers. With Rickey out of town on a scouting trip, Breadon contacted manager Rogers Hornsby to get his opinion on Alexander. Hornsby's reaction: Claim him.

Alexander turned out to be a great addition to the club— even before he struck out the Yankees' Tony Lazzeri to preserve the Cardinals' lead in the seventh inning of Game 7 of the World Series.

Because the Cardinals had never played in a World Series, St. Louisans didn't know exactly how to respond when the team came back to St. Louis after splitting the first two games of the Series with the Yankees in New York. But respond they did.

The *St. Louis Globe-Democrat* devoted its front page to

Babe Ruth stole second base on this play in Game 6—and he took down Cards shortstop Tommy Thevenow in the process. With two out in the ninth inning of Game 7 and St. Louis ahead, 3-2, Ruth attempted another steal and was nailed on catcher Bob O'Farrell's throw to second baseman Rogers Hornsby.

ST. LOUIS CARDINALS 1926 PENNANT WINNERS

DOUTHIT · WARWICK · O'FARRELL · VICK · SOUTHWORTH · HA[...] · KEEN · RHEM · HALLAHAN · ROGERS HORNSBY · ALEXANDER · SHERDEL · H. BELL · FLOWERS · TOPORCER · REINH[...] · [...]THORON · L. BELL · BOTTOMLEY · THEVENOW · HAINES

© PERSONS & CAVAGNARO ST. LOUIS

Game 3, punctuating its coverage with a banner headline that screamed: "GREATEST DEMONSTRATION IN CITY'S BASEBALL HISTORY STAGED AS FRENZIED MULTITUDES LIONIZE BASEBALL HEROES AMID BEDLAM OF NOISE AND JOYOUS ENTHUSIASM."

The Cardinals' triumph in Game 7 at Yankee Stadium touched off another major celebration that didn't end until long after the team's victory train had pulled back into Union Station from New York.

Of course, Southworth and Alexander weren't the only standouts on the '26 Cardinals. Besides Alexander, there were four other future Hall of Famers on the club—Hornsby, Jim Bottomley, Chick Hafey and Jesse Haines. Catcher Bob O'Farrell was the league's Most Valuable Player; Bottomley led the N.L. in RBIs and total bases; and pitcher Flint Rhem tied for the most wins in the N.L.

1931 World Series Champions

The 1931 season saw the emergence of a player who would turn out to be the sparkplug for the decade's great Gas House Gang teams: a 27-year-old outfielder named Pepper Martin, who previously had managed only 14 at-bats in the major leagues.

John Leonard Martin got his nickname in the minor leagues, and it stuck because it reflected his style on the field. He knew only one way to play—all out, all the time. Martin's uniform was always dirty.

The Oklahoma native took over the starting spot in center field in June—after the Cardinals dealt Taylor Douthit to Cincinnati—and St. Louis never looked back, easily winning its second consecutive pennant.

The Cardinals reached the 100-victory plateau for the first time in franchise history and became the first National League team to top the century mark in 18 years. They finished 13 games ahead of the second-place Giants.

Martin's play was inspiring to even older Cardinals players, like Frankie Frisch, who was named the league's MVP. Frisch led the Cardinals in only one major offensive statistical category, stolen bases (28, a league-leading total), but he was recognized for his steady play and leadership on a team that featured five future Hall of Famers.

As good as the regular lineup was—and the presence of Frisch, Chick Hafey, Jim Bottomley and Martin made it mighty good—the Cardinals were particularly dangerous because of deep starting pitching, led by lefthander Bill Hallahan, rookie Paul Derringer and veteran spitballer Burleigh Grimes. Hallahan tied for the league lead in wins, and the trio combined for 54 victories. Three other pitchers also

The Cardinals' Pepper Martin carried a big stick in the 1931 Series, collecting 12 hits against the A's. As reflected by his nickname, Martin was known for his all-out play.

were double-figure winners.

Martin, who from 1924 through 1930 spent most of his playing time in the minors, brought excitement to the team. He was always a prankster, once registering in a hotel as gangster Pretty Boy Floyd. The local sheriff wasn't amused.

Martin, who made one pinch-running appearance in the 1928 World Series after playing sparingly for the Cardinals in the regular season, was determined not to sit idly by in the 1931 Fall Classic. He didn't, either. Martin collected 12 hits, drove in five runs and stole five bases as the Cardinals upset the Philadelphia Athletics to win their second Series championship.

When commissioner Kenesaw Mountain Landis visited the Cardinals' clubhouse to offer his congratulations, he told Martin, "I'd rather trade places with you than any other man in the country."

Replied Martin: "That will be fine, Judge—if we can trade salaries, too."

Veteran Burleigh Grimes won 17 regular-season games in 1931 and Frankie Frisch (inset) was named the N.L.'s MVP. Grimes won twice in the World Series, taking Games 3 and 7.

1934 World Series Champions

Joe Medwick's hard slide into third baseman Marv Owen in Game 7 angered Detroit fans, who threw debris onto the field. Commissioner Kenesaw Mountain Landis met with manager Frankie Frisch (3) and Medwick, and he ordered Medwick out of the game.

After Frankie Frisch took over as Cardinals manager during the 1933 season, he was determined to mold the team in his style. Not only did he want players who were aggressive, but he wanted players who exhibited discipline and gave 100 percent effort at all times.

Starting in spring training in 1934, Frisch established strict rules that he wanted his players to follow—no drinking or gambling and a midnight curfew for players on the road. He wasn't dealing with a bunch of choir boys, either—not with such players as Pepper Martin and Dizzy Dean on the roster.

Dean wasn't about to let a new set of rules change his behavior. He was joined in some of his escapades in the summer of '34 by brother Paul, a rookie who proved to be a major addition to the rotation.

Upset about the prospect of taking a trip to Detroit to play an exhibition game in the middle of the pennant race, the

Having the Tigers by the tail was a happy experience for the Cardinals' Dizzy Dean, who found time to joke with humorist Will Rogers after breezing to a six-hit, 11-0 victory over Detroit in Game 7. St. Louis played without left fielder Medwick from the middle of the sixth inning on, but by that time Dean and the National League champs had a 9-0 lead.

Dean brothers intentionally missed the train. Frisch announced he was fining and suspending both players. That made the Deans even more irate, and it looked as if the brouhaha might upend the Cardinals' pennant hopes.

Dizzy even tore up two uniforms to show reporters and photographers his displeasure. After about a week, the entire dispute was settled—Paul was reinstated first, then Diz. It was just in time for the brothers to lead the Cardinals' charge to the pennant.

Dizzy became a 30-game winner by winning four times in the season's final 10 days. Paul threw a no-hitter on September 21 and posted 19 victories overall, enabling the duo to surpass Dizzy's spring-training prediction that the brothers would combine for 45 wins.

The surging Cardinals overcame a 5½-game deficit to the Giants with 17 games to play. The Cards clinched the pennant on the final day of the season, an afternoon on which Dizzy racked up win No. 30 by shutting out the Reds. Dean was named the league's MVP.

Waiting to play the Cardinals in the World Series were the Detroit Tigers, and Dean again was able to back up his prediction of a Cardinals victory—although Detroit did not go down meekly.

The Series went to Game 7, which forever will be remembered because of Joe Medwick's removal from the game after his hard slide into third base riled the Detroit crowd. With fans hurling bottles, fruit and vegetables onto the field in the sixth inning, commissioner Kenesaw Mountain Landis ordered Medwick out of the game. No matter. The Gas House Gang, with Dizzy Dean in full control, was en route to an 11-0 victory.

1942
World Series Champions

With the Cardinals trailing the Brooklyn Dodgers by 9½ games on the morning of August 16, general manager Branch Rickey probably had a lot of people agreeing with him when he lamented, "We don't have a chance."

Luckily for Rickey and the Cardinals, none of the people agreeing with him were St. Louis players.

Putting on one of the most incredible finishes in baseball history, manager Billy Southworth's 1942 Cardinals won 41 of their final 48 games and stormed to the National League pennant.

The Cards forged a first-place tie less than a month after facing that 9½-game deficit, then moved into first place—to stay—on September 13 when they split a doubleheader against the Phillies and the Dodgers lost two games to the Reds. St. Louis clinched the pennant on the final day of the season, completing a 20-4 September run. Brooklyn was 16-10 in the last month.

The Cardinals' 106 victories set a franchise record that still stands. There were myriad reasons for the team's success, starting with the pitching. The staff ERA of 2.55 was the lowest in the majors since 1919. Mort Cooper won 22 games, fashioned a 1.78 ERA and threw 10 shutouts. He was named the National League's MVP. Rookie Johnny Beazley went 21-6.

Cooper, who wore uniform No. 13, was stuck on 13 victories in 1942, so he switched to No. 14 and promptly got his 14th win. He then wore No. 15 and posted his 15th triumph, and on it went—all the way to 22.

The team's offense, while not posting overwhelming numbers, was solid. Stan Musial, playing his first full major league season, was the left fielder and batted .315. Gifted center fielder Terry Moore hit .288, and right fielder Enos Slaughter led the team with a .318 mark and also contributed team-

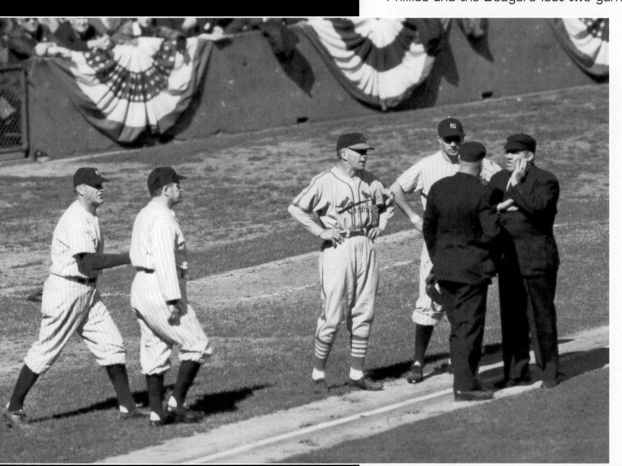

Manager Billy Southworth was outnumbered by Yankees and umpires in a 1942 Series dispute—but the scoreboard favored his Cardinals, who won in five games.

high totals of 13 home runs and 98 RBIs.

The left side of the infield, manned by standout shortstop Marty Marion and rookie Whitey Kurowski, was first-rate.

It was the youth of the team that prompted most observers to pick the Yankees to win the World Series. But Musial and company weren't awed by the New Yorkers and went out and proved it, winning the Fall Classic in five games. Kurowski provided the big moment, breaking a 2-2 tie in Game 5 with a Series-deciding two-run homer in the ninth inning.

After the clincher, winning pitcher Johnny Beazley (with glove) and batting star Whitey Kurowski (next to Beazley, facing camera) celebrated the Cards' title with Southworth and Harry Walker (both sitting), Enos Slaughter and Stan Musial.

DORRILL PHOTO

ST. LOUIS CARDINALS...1942

From the left, back row...FRANK CRESPI, COAKER TRIPLETT, ERVIN DUSAK, RAY SANDERS, TERRY MOORE, MAX LANIER, MORTON COOPER, HOWARD KRIST, MURRY DICKSON, LLOYD MOORE and BUTCH YATKEMAN, club-house attendant. Center row....DR. H.J. WEAVER, trainer; BILL BECKMANN, JIM BROWN, HARRY WALKER, JOHN BEAZLEY, ERNIE WHITE, ENOS SLAUGHTER, HARRY GUMBERT, HOWARD POLLET, WALKER COOPER, JOFF CROSS and LEO WARD, Secy. Front row...MARTY MARION, STAN MUSIAL, JOHNNY HOPP, Coach MIKE GONZALES, Manager BILLY SOUTHWORTH, Coach BUZZY WARES, GEORGE KUROWSKI, SAM NARRON and KEN O'DEA.

1944

World Series Champions

The Cardinals had won previous championships in almost every way possible—in a tight race, via a runaway, with outstanding hitting and because of overwhelming pitching. The story of the 1944 Cardinals was highlighted by a record-setting defense.

Led by shortstop Marty Marion, who had taken over as the team's veteran leader in the absence of Terry Moore, the Cardinals set a then-major league record with a .982 fielding percentage. Four St. Louis players led the National League in fielding at their positions—Marion, first baseman Ray Sanders, third baseman Whitey Kurowski and center fielder Johnny Hopp. Marion was named the league's Most Valuable Player, despite hitting only .267 with 63 runs batted in. Six players on his own team hit more home runs, six hit for a higher average and six drove in more runs, but to a man the Cards agreed Marion was the MVP.

Sanders drove in 102 runs, Hopp batted .336 and fast-emerging outfielder Stan Musial hit .347.

Another secret to the Cardinals' success was their ability to adequately replace all of their stars who had left for military service. Harry Walker, Lou Klein, Al Brazle, Howie Krist and Ernie White departed for duty before the season began, and Red Munger joined them in the middle of the year. Moore, Enos Slaughter and Johnny Beazley had left after the 1942 season.

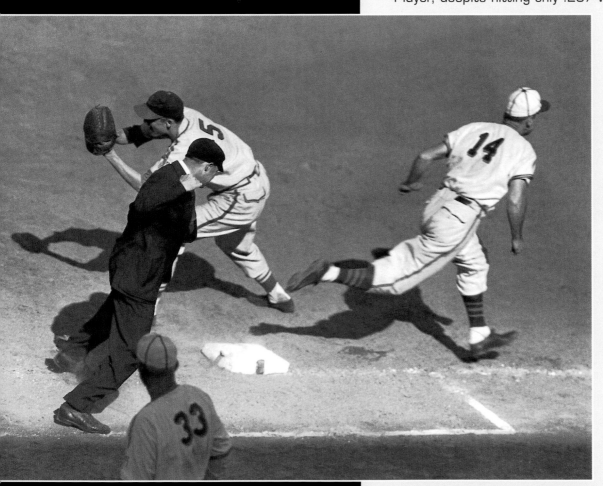

The Browns' Al Zarilla raced across first base in the fourth inning of Game 5 after hitting a ground ball to Cardinals pitcher Mort Cooper. Ray Sanders (5) already had taken Cooper's throw for the putout, and he quickly stepped off the bag.

Mort Cooper was a 22-game winner, Ted Wilks and Max Lanier each had 17 victories and Harry Brecheen won 16 games as the Cardinals finished with 105 wins for the second consecutive season. They had won 106 in 1942.

The Cardinals turned the pennant race into a rout in July, and they opened a 20-game lead by the end of August. Only a September slump—they lost 15 of 20 games in one stretch—kept them from challenging the league record of 116 wins.

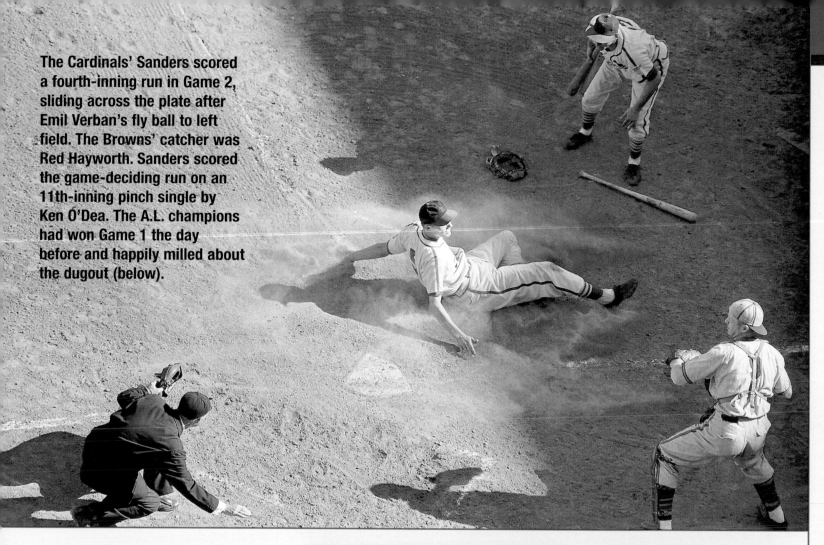

The Cardinals' Sanders scored a fourth-inning run in Game 2, sliding across the plate after Emil Verban's fly ball to left field. The Browns' catcher was Red Hayworth. Sanders scored the game-deciding run on an 11th-inning pinch single by Ken O'Dea. The A.L. champions had won Game 1 the day before and happily milled about the dugout (below).

The only suspense for the Cardinals was whom they would face in the World Series, and it turned out to be the St. Louis Browns, with whom they shared Sportsman's Park. The Browns would be making the only World Series appearance in franchise history.

Most baseball people thought postseason experience gave manager Billy Southworth and the Cardinals an advantage. The Browns proved tougher than expected in the Streetcar Series, though, winning two of the first three games. But starters Brecheen, Cooper and Lanier and reliever Wilks held the American Leaguers to two runs in the next three games—the N.L. champions won, 5-1, 2-0 and 3-1—and the Cardinals were World Series champions for the second time in three seasons.

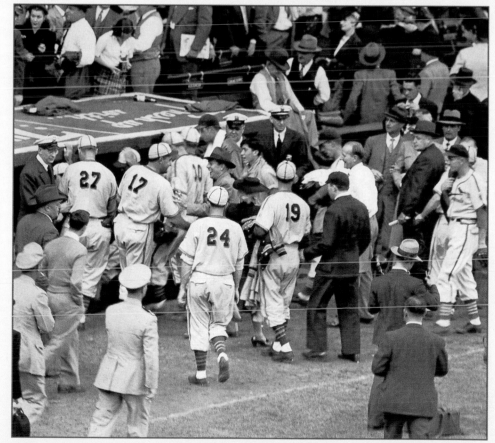

1946

World Series Champions

With their stars returning from military service, the Cardinals began the 1946 season with great expectations. Their fans were thinking the same way, and they turned out in record numbers. For the first time in franchise history, home attendance reached one million.

What no one knew was the obstacles that would have to be overcome for St. Louis to win its fourth pennant in five years. Pitchers Johnny Beazley and Ernie White returned from military service with arm injuries. In late May, the Mexican League raided the Cardinals, signing pitchers Max Lanier and Fred Martin and second baseman Lou Klein. And Red Barrett, who had won 21 games for the Cards in 1945, was ineffective.

Yet St. Louis persevered.

Klein's departure opened an infield spot for Red Schoendienst, who as a rookie in 1945 had played left field. Schoendienst became a fixture at second base. Stan Musial, who previously had been used exclusively in the outfield, saw extensive duty at first base in his return to the club after one year in the Navy. The year away didn't hurt Musial. He won the league's MVP award after lea[d]ing the National League in almost every major offensive category.

Enos Slaughter won the league'[s] RBI crown, and Whitey Kurowski batted .301.

As was the case for much of th[e]

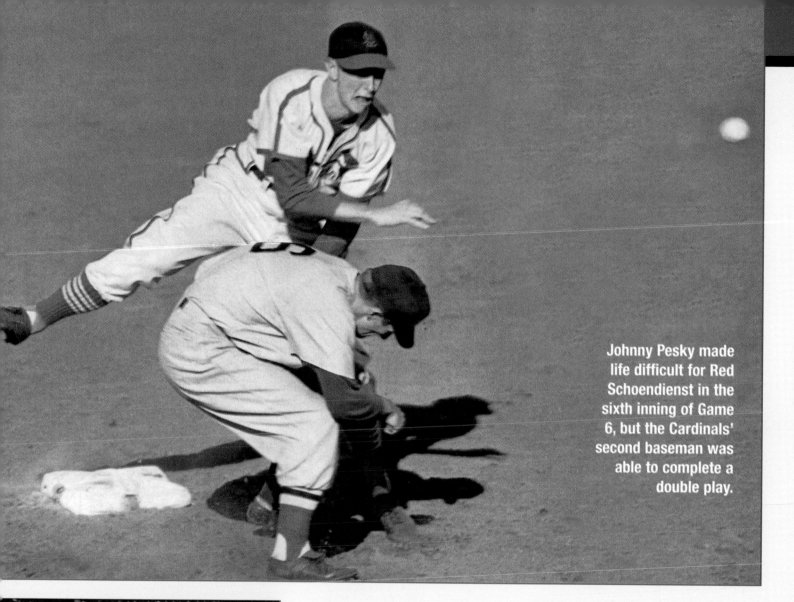

Johnny Pesky made life difficult for Red Schoendienst in the sixth inning of Game 6, but the Cardinals' second baseman was able to complete a double play.

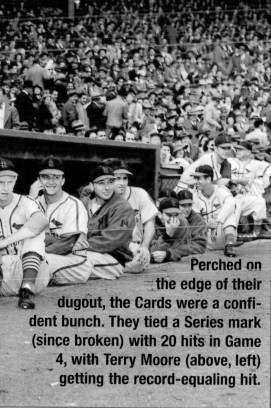

Perched on the edge of their dugout, the Cards were a confident bunch. They tied a Series mark (since broken) with 20 hits in Game 4, with Terry Moore (above, left) getting the record-equaling hit.

decade, the Cardinals battled Brooklyn for the pennant. On July 2, the Dodgers led by 7½ games; by July 18, the Cards had slipped into the lead, and it was nip and tuck the rest of the way.

Time and again, the teams were tied for first place, and that was the scenario on the final afternoon of the regular season. Former Cardinal Mort Cooper gave his old team a chance to win the pennant that day when, pitching for the Braves, he shut out the Dodgers. But the Cubs defeated manager Eddie Dyer's Cardinals, leaving Brooklyn and St. Louis tied with 96-58 records and forcing the first pennant play-off in major league history.

The format was a best-of-three series, and when the Dodgers won the coin flip, Brooklyn manager Leo Durocher asked that the first game be played in St. Louis, with the second and third game (if necessary) scheduled for Ebbets Field.

There was no third game. The Cardinals won, 4-2 and 8-4, and advanced to the World Series against the Red Sox, who had won their pennant race by 12 games. Harry Brecheen tossed a shutout in Game 2, allowed only one run in Game 6 and won in relief of Murry Dickson in Game 7 after Enos Slaughter's mad dash from first base on Harry Walker's eighth-inning hit provided the winning margin in a 4-3 victory.

1964
World Series Champions

Umpire Bill McKinley ruled that the Yankees' Joe Pepitone, checking his swing, was hit by this Bob Gibson pitch in the sixth inning of Game 2. Cards manager Johnny Keane and players Dick Groat and Tim McCarver (opposite page) argued the ball hit Pepitone's bat.

On the night of September 28, the Cardinals had five games to play in the 1964 season. St. Louis had climbed back into the National League pennant race—the club had been 6½ games behind the then-league-leading Phillies eight days earlier—but still was one game out of first place, now held by Cincinnati. Manager Johnny Keane didn't know what the outcome of the race would be, but he did know at least part of his own future.

Writing a letter in longhand, with his wife typing it on a borrowed typewriter, Keane crafted his resignation as manager of the Cardinals. He tucked the letter in his pocket, ready to deliver it to owner August A. Busch Jr. as soon as the Cardinals' season ended.

Little did Keane know the season would last another 2½ weeks, until the Cardinals defeated the Yankees in Game 7 of the World Series. The result didn't change Keane's mind, however, and he announced his resignation the day after the Series ended. Keane had been upset with reports earlier in the season that Busch was preparing to fire him and hire Leo Durocher as manager, and he also was unhappy with the mid-August firing of general manager Bing Devine.

Keane's resignation was almost as shocking as the Cardinals' come-from-behind spurt to win the pennant. Only the true believers among Cardinals fans thought the team could pull it out. But an eight-game winning streak by St. Louis, 10 consecutive losses by the Phillies and four Cincinnati defeats in the Reds' last five games put the Cardinals in position to win the pennant on the final day of the season.

The turning point in the World Series came in the sixth inning of Game 4. The Yankees led the Series, two games to one, and were ahead, 3-0, in this game. Another win and the Yankees would have a commanding lead in the Series. After the Cardinals loaded the bases against Al Downing, team captain Ken Boyer pulled St. Louis ahead by hammering a pitch into the left-field seats. With Roger Craig and Ron Taylor contributing 8⅔ innings of two-hit, scoreless relief, the Cards won the game and evened the Series.

Boyer, the National League's MVP that season, later called

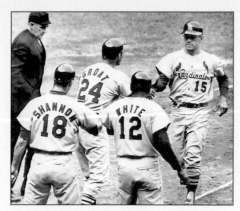

St. Louis' McCarver (left, sliding past Yankees catcher Elston Howard) showed he could run the bases—and that he was capable of breaking into a home run trot, too. He won Game 5 with a three-run shot in the 10th inning and found a welcoming committee at home plate.

the grand slam the highlight of his career. As he rounded third base, he passed younger brother Clete, playing third base for the Yankees. It was all Clete could do to keep himself from smiling.

After the teams split the next two games—Tim McCarver's three-run homer in the 10th won Game 5—the Cardinals turned to Bob Gibson for Game 7, and he carried a 6-0 lead into the sixth before hanging on for a 7-5 victory. He struck out nine Yankees in a game that gave the Cards their first World Series crown since 1946.

World Series Champions

The acquisition of outfielder Roger Maris from the Yankees proved to be the final piece to the Cardinals' puzzle for 1967. Now strong at all positions, they marched to the National League pennant, moving into first place to stay in June and eventually winning by 10½ games over the Giants.

The addition of Maris allowed Mike Shannon to move from right field to third base, solidifying the lineup and adding winning experience to a team already primed for a big season.

First baseman Orlando Cepeda, obtained from the Giants a year earlier, batted .325 with 25 home runs and 111 RBIs and won the league's Most Valuable Player award. Also powering El Birdos' offense were outfielders Lou Brock and Curt Flood and catcher Tim McCarver.

The pitching staff proved to be just as effective, despite losing Bob Gibson for nearly two months because of a broken leg, suffered when he was hit by a line drive off the bat of the Pirates' Roberto Clemente.

Dick Hughes, a 29-year-old rookie,

came out of nowhere and won 16 games, and young Nellie Briles took Gibson's spot in the rotation and won his last nine decisions. Another promising pitcher, lefthander Steve Carlton, won five games while Gibson was out and finished 14-9. The trio of Hughes, Briles and Carlton combined for 44 victories, easing the absence of Gibson.

When Gibson was hurt on July 15, the Cardinals were nursing a four-game lead and many thought their season would unravel. But the steady hand of manager Red Schoendienst helped make certain that didn't happen. In fact, when Gibson returned to the mound on September 7, the Cardinals' lead had grown to 11½ games. Without their ace, the Cards had gone 36-20.

The easy pennant run didn't leave the Cardinals overconfident for the World Series against the Red Sox, who featured a Triple Crown winner in outfielder Carl Yastrzemski and an ace pitcher of their own in Jim Lonborg.

The Red Sox's 1967 regular season had been called the "The Impossible Dream"—Boston had finished in ninth place in 1966— but the phrase took on another meaning in the World Series. Gibson (three complete-game victories and a home run in Game 7), Brock (.414 average and seven stolen bases), Maris (.385) and the rest of the Cardinals made sure that Boston's dream of winning the Series was just that—impossible.

Bob Gibson (top, left photo), Orlando Cepeda (30) and their teammates had that championship feeling. Gibson went 3-0 in the Series with a 1.00 ERA. Lou Brock (left) scored eight runs and stole seven bases.

1982
World Series Champions

A new word was added to baseball's lexicon in 1982—Whiteyball. The definition of the word was provided by the Cardinals themselves, who collectively played with a style and strategy that most people weren't accustomed to seeing. While longtime Orioles manager Earl Weaver, for one, preferred to wait for a three-run homer, Cardinals manager Whitey Herzog and his bunch didn't wait for anything to happen—they made it happen.

The '82 Cardinals ran at every opportunity, and they scooted all the way to the National League pennant and World Series championship. The accomplishment was particularly rewarding for Series first-timer Herzog, whose Kansas City Royals had lost three times in American League Championship Series matchups against the Yankees in the 1970s.

With his team playing in spacious Busch Stadium, Herzog knew the Cardinals couldn't out-slug their opponents. So he built a team that relied on speed, offensively and defensively, and kept constant pressure on opponents, hoping to force them into mistakes. The Cards often scored without the benefit of a hit, turning a walk, a stolen base, a ground ball and a sacrifice fly into a "rally."

"Small ball," it turned out, would ignite the Cardinals to three pennants in a six-year span.

Only one player hit more than 12 home runs for the '82 Cards—right fielder George Hendrick, who finished with 19—and the team total of 67 homers was the lowest in the major leagues. The club stole a National League-leading 200 bases, and combined with the best defense in the league and a pitching staff that allowed the fewest runs in the N.L., it was easy to see why Herzog's formula paid off.

The infield of Keith Hernandez, Tommy Herr, Ozzie Smith (acquired from San Diego) and Ken Oberkfell combined for only 44 errors. Bob Forsch and Joaquin Andujar led the pitching staff with 15 wins each, and Bruce Sutter was baseball's most dominant closer, saving 36 games. Two rookies, Dave LaPoint and John Stuper, pitched effectively, as did Steve Mura, obtained in another Herzog trade with the Padres.

Some of the off-field moves engineered by Herzog in his dual role as manager and general manager paid huge dividends. Ozzie Smith came over in a trade for fellow shortstop Garry Templeton and immediately flashed the wizardry that would amaze teammates, rivals and fans into the mid-1990s. Lonnie Smith was obtained from the Indians in a three-team deal and became the quality leadoff hitter the Cardinals needed to make their attack work.

The Cardinals also got a little lucky, as happens to most good teams. When center fielder David Green was sidelined with a hamstring injury in May, St. Louis summoned an unknown player from the minor leagues and told him he likely would be in the majors for just a few weeks—until Green was healthy again. The call-up, Willie McGee, wound up staying for nearly a decade (and later returned to the club), becoming one of the franchise's most popular and successful players.

A 12-game winning streak in April convinced the Cardinals they were good enough to win, and the stable starting pitching and the presence of Sutter in the bullpen kept the team from a prolonged losing streak. In fact, the Cards never lost more than three consecutive games until the last week of the season—after they had wrapped up the East Division title.

George Hendrick collected three of his nine Series hits in Game 5 at Milwaukee.

If the Cardinals had any doubts that 1982 was going to be their year, they were erased on a Sunday afternoon in August when third-string catcher Glenn Brummer—not exactly one of the team's speedsters—stole home with two out in the 12th inning of a game against the Giants at Busch.

Most St. Louis fans still remember where they were when Brummer made his startling game-winning steal—just like they recall what they were doing when Smith and Jack Clark hit dramatic playoff homers three years later.

"A guy told me he was listening on the radio and drove off the highway," Brummer said. "Another guy told me he was barbecuing and knocked his grill over. I guess it shocked them so much they haven't forgotten."

Thus inspired, the Cardinals went on to clinch the division title and prepared for their first postseason berth in 14 years. Their opponent in the N.L. Championship Series was not determined until the last day of the regular season, when Atlanta clinched the West Division crown—thanks to a final-game loss by the second-place Dodgers.

The Cardinals were losing the NLCS opener to the Braves' Phil Niekro, 1-0, when rain halted the game two outs before it would have become official. After a long delay, the game was postponed. Whether that was

Bruce Sutter got the glad hand from manager Whitey Herzog after saving Game 3. Ozzie Smith (left, sliding) scored three runs, had five hits and played errorless ball in his first World Series.

divine intervention or not, the Cards went on to sweep the Braves and advanced to the World Series against the Milwaukee Brewers.

It was fitting, perhaps, that the Cardinals and Brewers emerged to play in the Series since Herzog, in his G.M. days, had conducted some major business with Milwaukee. He had traded Rollie Fingers and long-time Cardinals favorite Ted Simmons, among others, to the Brewers. Herzog, who gave up his front-office role in April 1982, joked that he should have been named "general manager of the year"—in Milwaukee.

No one in St. Louis was laughing after Game 1 of the World Series, a 10-0 romp for the Brewers, but the

Cardinals rebounded. Getting spectacular all-around play from McGee, key hitting from catcher Darrell Porter and Hernandez and standout pitching from Joaquin Andujar, Stuper and Sutter, St. Louis forced a seventh game. The Cards won the finale, 6-3, thanks to a three-run rally in the sixth inning capped by Hendrick's go-ahead single. Sutter provided St. Louis with one of its greatest baseball moments when he struck out Gorman Thomas to end the Series.

Herzog was happy for all of his players, but especially for those he had worked so hard to bring to St. Louis, like Porter, who had been with him in Kansas City and had fought back from alcohol and drug abuse. Porter was named the MVP of both the NLCS and World Series.

He also was happy for team owner Gussie Busch, who had given Herzog the freedom he needed to build the team and had been rewarded with another championship.

Herzog and the Cardinals thought they had been cheated out of the division title a year earlier in a strike-interrupted season. Even though they had the best overall record in the division, they didn't win either half of the split season and thereby didn't qualify for the playoffs. Winning the 1982 World Series eased the frustration—mightily.

2004

Truth be told, Cardinals fans entered the 2004 season with modest hopes. To have a chance in the last week of the season would be fine. Well, maybe not *fine*, but to count on anything more would have been floating in fantasy.

All the talk in the National League's Central Division was about the Cubs and the Astros. Or the Astros and the Cubs.

The idea that the Cardinals would win 105 games—which they did—was preposterous. That the Cardinals would win the division by 13 games—which they did—was unthinkable. A trip to the World Series? You can't be serious.

That was the kind of perspective Cardinals fans needed on October 27 as the Boston Red Sox celebrated somewhere in the vicinity of the pitching mound at Busch Stadium. The Cardinals, done in by a pitching staff that ran out of fumes and by a most inopportune scoring drought (could there be a worse combination?), were swept in the World Series. But that in no way should be the lasting image of the 2004 season.

Jim Edmonds' 12th-inning homer in Game 6
of the NLCS sent fans into a frenzy and kept
St. Louis' World Series hopes alive.

Better to remember Jim Edmonds' walk-off home run in Game 6 of the National League Championship Series and game-saving diving catch in Game 7 than his 1-for-15 (a bunt single!) in the World Series.

Better to remember Scott Rolen's home run off Roger Clemens in Game 7 of the NLCS and his torrid MVP-type first half of the season than his 0-for-15 in the World Series.

Better to remember the surprise of Chris Carpenter's 15-win production after he missed the 2003 season because of shoulder surgery than the lack-of-hope stare as he sat out the World Series because of a freak arm injury.

Better to remember Albert Pujols' fourth straight magnificent season than the hobbled warrior who gutted it out through September and October on a painful foot that made every stretch and every swing a test of courage.

Better to remember a better-than-advertised starting rotation that had four 15-game winners—Carpenter, Matt Morris, Jeff Suppan and Jason Marquis—than the Band-Aid bunch that seemed forever one out—one pitch, even—from escaping the Red Sox's powerful lineup.

Better to remember Jason Isringhausen's club record-tying 47 saves during the regular season than the fact he was used once in the World Series—as a mop-up man (the Cardinals were never ahead).

Far, far better to remember the Cardinals' magnificent rush to the National League pennant as they became the talk of baseball than the way it ended.

It was by most any measure a stellar season. The start matched the predictions (and Redbirds fans' fears): 23-22 on May 26. For the next three months, the Cardinals metamorphosed into a runaway train. From May 31 through September 5 they were 66-21, a .759 clip. During the Cardinals' three-game sweep of the Royals in June, which helped contribute to St. Louis' 11-1 interleague record, Kansas City manager Tony Pena said, "This is the best ballclub we've faced. They just kicked us around." Atlanta's Chipper Jones called the Cardinals "the Yankees of the Midwest," and Milwaukee's Geoff Jenkins claimed St. Louis had a "Nintendo lineup."

Because it was so unexpected, it truly did feel like a magical season for the 2004 St. Louis Cardinals—certainly one to remember.

Clockwise from top left: Chris Carpenter, Jason Isringhausen, Albert Pujols and Scott Rolen, who were key components of the 16th Cardinals team to capture the N.L. pennant.

1928, 1930, 1943, 1968, 1985, 1987

Bob Gibson dazzled in the 1968 World Series against Detroit, but the Cardinals blew a three games-to-one lead. A misjudged fly ball in Game 7 was disastrous for St. Louis.

Close. Very close.

Seven times the Cardinals have won the National League pennant but failed to win the World Series. On two of those occasions, a different outcome on one play might have changed the Series outcome. Another time, victory also seemed within the Cards' grasp.

In 1968, the Cardinals and Detroit Tigers went to Game 7 of the World Series, Bob Gibson matched against Mickey Lolich. The game was scoreless until the seventh inning, when the Tigers put two runners on with two out. Jim Northrup then hit a smash to center field, a drive that Curt Flood normally would have caught easily. This time, he misjudged the ball—he broke in and the ball sailed past him—and it went for a triple. Northrup scored on Bill Freehan's double, and the Tigers parlayed the 3-0 lead into a 4-1 victory.

In 1985, the telling moment came in Game 6 of the Series against the Kansas City Royals. With the Cardinals one win from the championship, the game was scoreless until the eighth inning, when pinch hitter Brian Harper's RBI single gave St. Louis the lead. That edge held until the bottom of the ninth, when a missed call by first-base umpire Don Denkinger—pinch hitter Jorge Orta was ruled safe on an inning-opening grounder on which replays clearly showed he was out—helped the Royals rally for a 2-1 victory. The winning runs scored on a one-out single by former Cardinal Dane Iorg.

Inspired, the Royals blasted the Cardinals, 11-0, in Game 7 to capture the Series.

Todd Worrell (38) disputed Don Denkinger's call in Game 6 of the '85 Series. In Game 7, Joaquin Andujar (above, pointing) was ejected. Below are Whitey Herzog, Terry Pendleton, Ozzie Smith, Tommy Herr and Jack Clark.

Two years later, in 1987, the Cardinals found themselves in the same position—with a chance to win the Series in Game 6, this time against the Minnesota Twins. St. Louis was leading, 5-2, in that game, but Gary Gaetti's double and Don Baylor's two-run homer in the fifth inning tied the score and, after the Twins slipped ahead later in that inning, Kent Hrbek followed with a grand slam off Ken Dayley in the sixth. The Twins won, 11-5.

Unlike 1985, Game 7 wasn't a blowout, but the Twins prevailed, 4-2, and became the first team in history to take the World Series by winning all four games at home and none on the road.

The Cardinals' other four World Series losses

were painful, but not in such an agonizing "what if" way. The Cards were swept by the Yankees in 1928 and by the Red Sox in 2004, lost in six games to the Philadelphia A's in 1930 and fell in five games to the Yankees in 1943.

Four times the Cardinals have advanced to the National League playoffs but lost in their bid for the pennant. St.

Louis was defeated in seven games by the Atlanta Braves in the 1996 N.L. Championship Series (after the Cards had taken a 3-1 lead), lost in five games to the New York Mets in the 2000 NLCS, came up short in decisive Game 5 of the 2001 Division Series against the Arizona Diamondbacks and fell to the San Francisco Giants, four games to one, in the 2002 NLCS.

Jim Bottomley (left) and the Cardinals were swept by Babe Ruth and the Yankees in the 1928 World Series. Stan Musial (opposite page, bottom) and company fell to Charlie Keller and the Yanks in the 1943 Series, a five-game Fall Classic in which Marty Marion homered in Game 2 (below) and was met at home plate by Mort Cooper (13). Manager Gabby Street (far right, top) saw his 1930 Cards lose to Connie Mack and the Athletics in a six-game Series in which St. Louis' Charley Gelbert (immediate right, top) and Chick Hafey (sliding) scored runs in Game 4.

The
STARTING LINEUP

MANAGER

10

He came to St. Louis in October 1995 with a managerial resume that had to be admired. Yet, admiration wasn't the only thing awaiting him. There also was skepticism from many who viewed him as an "American League manager."

He has been received coolly in some corners for reasons ranging from his offseason residence in California to the perception that he relies too much on statistics and not enough on instincts. And when Cardinals playoff teams of 1996, 2000, '01 and '02 failed to make the World Series, Tony La Russa received much of the heat.

Despite all of that, La Russa slowly has been embraced more tightly during his decade-long tenure in St. Louis. He won many over in 2002 by keeping the Cardinals steady during a season in which popular starting pitcher Darryl Kile died in June.

And his support soared in '04, when the Cardinals won 105 games in the regular season, then beat the Dodgers and Astros in the playoffs to bring the World Series to St. Louis for the first time since 1987. Another 100-win season in 2005 solidified his standing.

Through the years, fans have gained an appreciation for La Russa's respect for the game, for his pleadings to play with passion each and every day. Baseball, to La Russa, is a way of life. And that's something Cardinals fans can appreciate.

ALBERT PUJOLS

FIRST BASE
1.57

A spring training injury to Bobby Bonilla created an opportunity for Albert Pujols to break camp with the Cardinals in 2001 despite a resume that showed only one season of minor league experience. Instead of settling for a taste of major league pitching, Pujols devoured it, hitting so well that he never would see the minor leagues again.

A natural-born hitter, Pujols—thanks to his balance and quick wrists—is able to wait until the very last moment before unleashing a powerful yet controlled swing. He rarely looks fooled, and he hits the ball to all fields—with authority.

Pujols produces with a consistency that truly is rare. His lowest career average for a month is .319, his figure for May. He thrives against lefthanders and righthanders, at home and on the road, day and night. He is a .337 hitter with runners in scoring position. Pujols' walks have increased each season, and his strikeout totals declined each year through 2004 before rising slightly in 2005. Oh, and his average season in his first five years: .332, 40 homers, 124 RBIs.

In a young career loaded with highlights, Pujols' 2004 NLCS performance stands out. In a seven-game triumph over the Astros, Pujols went 14-for-28 with four home runs, nine RBIs and four walks.

ROGERS HORNSBY

SECOND BASE

No player in franchise history can match the hitting exploits of Rogers Hornsby, who batted .359 in 1,580 games as a Cardinal. Hornsby won six consecutive batting titles while playing for the Cards, three of those crowns coming when he hit .401, .424 and .403 in a four-year span. He later won a seventh batting championship as a member of the Boston Braves. His season hits totals as a Cardinals player included such figures as 250, 235 and 227. Anything but a singles hitter, he led the National League in doubles four times and in home runs twice. Hornsby and Ted Williams are the major leagues' only two-time Triple Crown winners—Hornsby was the National League's batting average/RBI/homer king in 1922 and 1925. Hornsby was player/manager for St. Louis' first World Series champions, the 1926 Cardinals.

THE RAJAH

THIRD BASE

KEN BOYER

Captain of the Cardinals in the early 1960s, Ken Boyer demonstrated his many leadership skills in 1964 when he helped St. Louis to its first World Series crown in 18 years. Boyer won MVP honors that season with a 24-homer, 119-RBI performance. In the Series, he delivered a momentum-turning grand slam in Game 4. A five-time Gold Glove winner who started four consecutive All-Star Games (and played in 10), the highly professional Boyer had the respect not only of his teammates but of everyone in baseball. He batted higher than .300 five times, with his career-best mark of .329 coming in 1961. He ranks second to Stan Musial on the Cardinals' all-time home run list with 255.

SHORTSTOP

WIZARD

OZZIE SMITH

What Rogers Hornsby and Stan Musial were to offense, Ozzie Smith was to defense. As a Cardinal, Smith won 11 consecutive Gold Gloves beginning in 1982 and topped National League shortstops in fielding percentage seven times. Smith, who batted .211 for San Diego in 1979, made himself into a highly capable offensive player. In 1987, he helped the Cards to their third World Series appearance in six seasons with his airtight defense (only 10 errors) and solid offense (.303 average and 75 RBIs). Playing with a flair afield and exhibiting a keen insight into how all facets of the game should be played, Smith rates as one of the most popular players in Cardinals history. Besides his many fielding records, he is sixth on the franchise's all-time hits list and third among Cards basestealers.

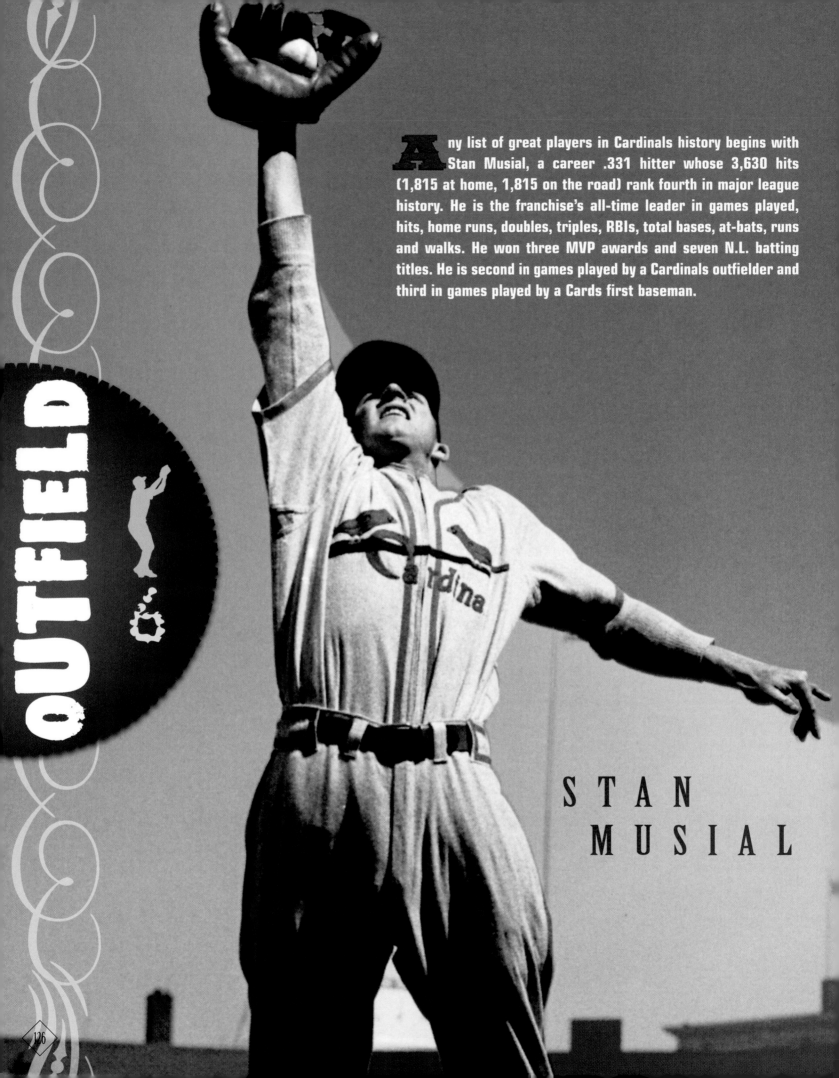

Any list of great players in Cardinals history begins with Stan Musial, a career .331 hitter whose 3,630 hits (1,815 at home, 1,815 on the road) rank fourth in major league history. He is the franchise's all-time leader in games played, hits, home runs, doubles, triples, RBIs, total bases, at-bats, runs and walks. He won three MVP awards and seven N.L. batting titles. He is second in games played by a Cardinals outfielder and third in games played by a Cards first baseman.

STAN MUSIAL

THE MAN

OUTFIELD
20

LOU
BROCK

ou Brock provided the spark at the top of the lineup that ignited the Cardinals to three pennants and two World Series titles in the 1960s. He led the National League in stolen bases eight times and established major league season and career steals records (both since broken). He is St. Louis' all-time steals leader and ranks No. 2 behind Stan Musial in six Cardinals career offensive categories—games played, runs, hits, total bases, at-bats and doubles. In 21 World Series games, he hit .391 and stole 14 bases.

Lou Brock

OUTFIELD

ENOS SLAUGHTER

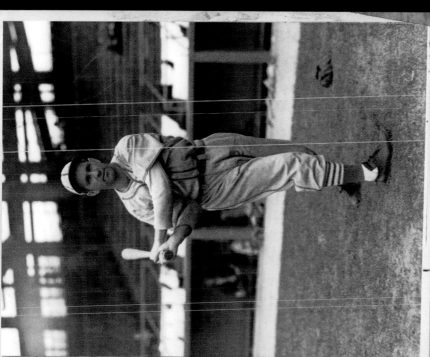

Enos Slaughter played in 10 All-Star Games, and he batted .381 in the midsummer classic. "Country" hit .305 in his 13 seasons as a Cardinal, and he fashioned a .300 mark overall in 19 years as a major leaguer. Slaughter ranks in the top five in most offensive categories in Cardinals history. He is second only to Stan Musial in RBIs despite missing three prime years because of military service. And, of course, he will live forever in Cardinals lore because of his World Series-winning sprint around the bases in the 1946 World Series against the Boston Red Sox.

CATCHER

23

Ted Simmons' first full season as the Cardinals' No. 1 catcher was 1971, and his .304 average that season proved he could swing the bat. Simmons batted .300 or higher six times in 10 years of regular catching duty for St. Louis, a span in which he averaged 90 runs batted in and five times hit 20 or more home runs. He holds Cardinals records for most home runs and RBIs in a season by a catcher, hitting 26 homers in 1979 and driving in 96 runs in 1972. Simmons actually had two 100-RBI seasons for the Cards—1974 and 1975, years in which he also played at other positions. In '75, he finished second in the National League batting race with a career-high .332 mark. He appeared in three All-Star Games and was a member of the N.L. team six times overall.

TED
SIMMONS

133

RH PITCHER 45

BOB GIBSON

There is little argument about Bob Gibson's ranking as the greatest Cardinals pitcher of all time. He won 251 games, put together five 20-victory seasons, captured two Cy Young Awards and one Most Valuable Player honor, pitched a no-hitter and recorded 3,117 strikeouts. In 1968, he set a major league record for lowest ERA, 300 or more innings pitched, finishing with a figure of 1.12. When games mattered the most, he came up big. Gibson compiled a 7-2 record in nine World Series starts and pitched eight complete games. His Series ERA was 1.89, and he struck out 92 batters in 81 innings. Seventeen of his strikeouts came in Game 1 of the 1968 Series. Gibson also won nine Gold Gloves.

LH PITCHER

HARRY BRECHEEN

onsistency was the trademark of Harry "The Cat" Brecheen, who didn't reach the majors to stay until he was 28 years old but won 127 games in 10 full seasons with the Cardinals. From 1944 through 1949, Brecheen posted at least 14 victories each season. He was outstanding in 1948, winning 20 games and leading the National League in ERA (2.24), strikeouts (149) and shutouts (seven). His career winning percentage as a Cardinal was .617. He became the first lefthander to win three games in a World Series, accomplishing the feat in 1946 when he pitched two complete-game victories against the Red Sox and then won in relief in Game 7. His nickname derived from his cat-quick fielding skills.

fig.1 *Split-finger Fastball*

BRUCE SUTTER

There was no question about what was coming when relief pitcher extraordinaire Bruce Sutter was on the mound. The only uncertainty was whether the batter would be able to hit the pitch, a split-finger fastball. More often than not, Sutter came out the winner in the confrontation—and so did the Cardinals. In his four seasons with St. Louis, Sutter led the National League in saves three times (with a high of 45 in 1984). In the Cards' 1982 World Series championship season, he recorded 36 saves and got the final out in the Series by striking out Milwaukee's Gorman Thomas.

The
Cardinals-Cubs
RIVALRY

Every winter, when the major league schedule is released for the upcoming season, certain games immediately draw attention.

For fans in St. Louis and Chicago, it's the no-holds-barred confrontations between the Cardinals and the Cubs.

Longtime Cardinal Rogers Hornsby (top) didn't look quite right in a Cubs uniform. Outfielders Max Flack (below left) and Cliff Heathcote switched teams between games of a doubleheader.

Whether the scene is Busch Stadium or Wrigley Field, the rivalry is hot and heavy—not only between the teams, but their fans as well. And as soon as the schedule is made public, fans in each city gobble up tickets for Cardinals-Cubs games in their home parks—and for pilgrimages to the rival city. Thousands of fans make the trip up and down Interstate 55 for Cards-Cubs series each year—and some even pile into the car three times in the course of a season.

It is not unusual to see Wrigley Field bleacherites wearing T-shirts reading "I cheer for two teams, the Cubs and whoever is playing the Cardinals." At Busch Stadium, the message is reversed. There are almost as many fans decked out in blue as there are red in St. Louis, and the opposite is true in Chicago.

Fans from each town are well versed in the baseball lore of the other city, and they don't hesitate to point out the other team's shortcomings over and over again.

Cardinals fans know all about the exploits of Ernie Banks, Billy Williams, Ferguson Jenkins, Ryne Sandberg, Sammy Sosa, Mark Prior and Derrek Lee—and Hack Wilson, Stan Hack and Phil Cavarretta, for that matter. Cubs fans are all too familiar with Stan Musial, Bob Gibson, Ken Boyer, Ozzie Smith, Mark McGwire, Jim Edmonds and Albert Pujols—and Dizzy Dean, Joe Medwick and Enos Slaughter, too.

St. Louis fans will tell you why they have a strong dislike for catcher Steve Swisher, even though he spent some time in a Cardinals uniform. Playing for the Cubs against the Pirates on the final day of the 1974 season, Swisher was charged with a ninth-inning passed ball that enabled Pittsburgh, trying to fight off the Cards for the East Division title, to tie the game. The Pirates then won in the 10th inning, clinching the division crown. A Pirates loss would have given the Cardinals a chance to force a tie for first place.

Cardinals fans still bemoan—and Cubs fans continue to cheer—that June day in 1984 when Sandberg hit two home runs off Bruce Sutter, one that tied the game in the ninth inning and another that deadlocked it in the 10th. Almost no one remembers that St. Louis' Willie McGee hit for the cycle in the same game, which the Cubs won in 11 innings.

No one on either side could tell you that the Cubs were making a big mistake when they traded Lou Brock to the

Changing allegiances in the Cards-Cubs rivalry is unheard of—well, almost. Broadcaster Harry Caray managed to make the switch in the course of calling Cardinals games for 25 years and Cubs games for 16 seasons.

Gas House Gang member Leo Durocher went on to manage the Cubs, a franchise that has never gotten over its 1964 trade of Lou Brock to the Cardinals.

Cardinals in a six-player deal in 1964, with pitcher Ernie Broglio the principal player going to Chicago. Brock, of course, turned into a Hall of Famer and Broglio hurt his arm and won only seven games for the Cubs in three years. Fans of both teams reflect on the deal as fate—the kind that more often than not has favored the Cardinals.

Cubs-Cardinals settings have been emotional—none more so than what occurred on June 22, 2002, when Cubs catcher Joe Girardi stepped to a microphone and told the Wrigley Field crowd there had been a "tragedy in the Cardinals family." Soon, the stunned fans learned that St. Louis pitcher Darryl Kile had been found dead in his Chicago hotel room that morning.

Baseball history has been a kinder, more frequent visitor to Cubs-Cards games. Musial collected his 3,000th career hit at Wrigley Field. Brock's 3,000th bounded off the hand of the Cubs' Dennis Lamp at Busch Stadium. Mark McGwire's record-breaking 62nd homer was against Chicago's Steve Trachsel at Busch.

There were epic pitching duels between Hall of Famers Gibson and Jenkins. Sutter and Lee Smith saved games for both teams, and Rogers Hornsby showed his extraordinary batting prowess both as a Cardinal and a Cub. Harry Caray was a legend in both broadcasting booths.

Cubs-Cards meetings also have been fodder for trivia. Musial made his lone pitching appearance in the majors—he faced one batter—in a 1952 game against the Cubs. Between games of a 1922 Chicago-St. Louis doubleheader, the clubs swapped outfielders. Cliff Heathcote played for the Cardinals in the first game and was in the Cubs' lineup in the nightcap. Max Flack was a Cub in the opener, a Cardinal in the second game.

The St. Louis-Chicago rivalry really took root in the 1940s. People became more transient after World War II, and it was not uncommon to take trips from one city to the other. The ever-expanding radio broadcasts of both teams also increased the clubs' popularity—and in turn fueled the rivalry. Fans became more familiar with the personnel on the rival club.

The Cardinals' biggest rivals on the field during the '40s were the Dodgers, because the two teams often battled for first place. But that rivalry never was as intense for the fans as the St. Louis-Chicago matchup.

The Cubs, who had won four pennants from 1929 through 1938, were evolving into lovable losers—big teddy bears that you could cuddle up with but seldom had to fear. They won the National League pennant in 1945, yes, but the franchise has had a mostly dismal history ever since. Cardinals fans poke fun at the Cubs' inability to reach the World Series—they came agonizingly close in 2003 but still haven't made it since '45—and take delight in noting the North Siders haven't won a Series since 1908.

Broadcaster Al Hrabosky, a former Cardinals

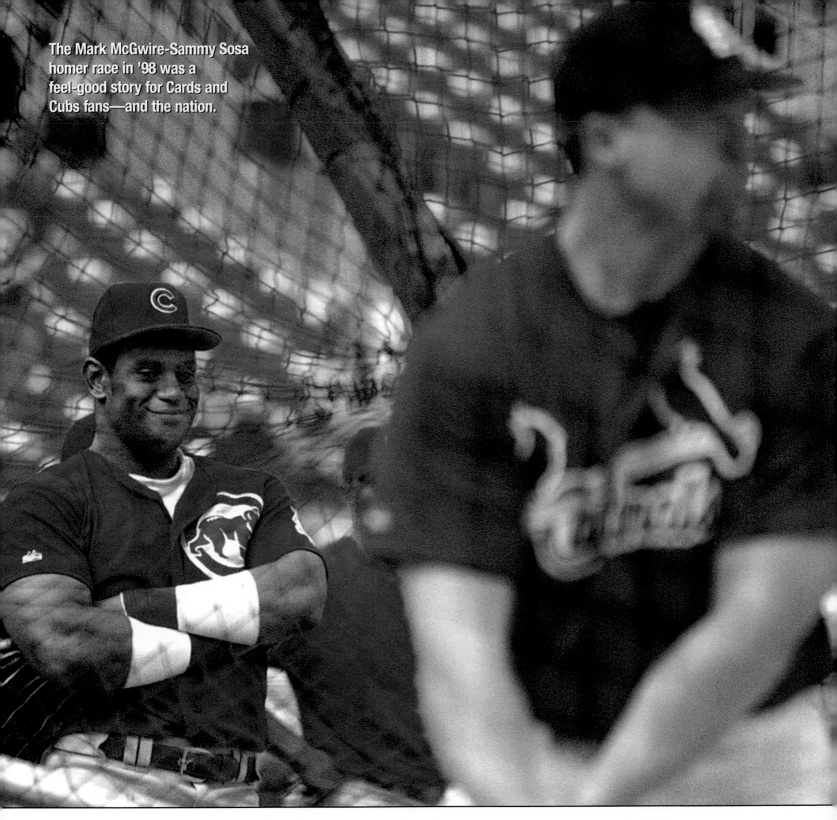

The Mark McGwire-Sammy Sosa homer race in '98 was a feel-good story for Cards and Cubs fans—and the nation.

pitcher, regularly points out that any team can have a bad century. Cubs fans can't counter with similar barbs. The Cardinals have won four World Series and eight pennants since 1945, and they had the satisfaction of clinching the 2005 N.L. Central title at Wrigley Field.

One person who had to learn to root for the Cubs and not the Cardinals was Caray, the voice of the Cards for 25 seasons. Caray spent the last 16 years of his life cheering openly for the Cubs as their lead broadcaster. "Holy Cow!"

was transformed into "Cubs win! Cubs win!"—but not often enough to please the Bleacher Bums.

Caray and the fans in Chicago and St. Louis haven't been the only ones affected by the fierce rivalry. Consider the households in central Illinois, many almost equidistant from Chicago and St. Louis. There, it is not unusual to find two people in a family cheering for the Cardinals and two pulling for the Cubs. In Champaign, Peoria, Decatur and other towns across the state, wagers are

On June 22, 2002, Cubs catcher Joe Girardi told the crowd at Wrigley Field there had been a "tragedy in the Cardinals family" and that the game was called off. Fans soon heard the shocking news: Darryl Kile had died.

won or lost and friendships made or broken because of the results of Cardinals-Cubs games.

Often, there has been nothing more significant than pride riding on the outcome of a particular Cardinals-Cubs game or series. One notable exception was in 1935, when the Cubs and Cards battled for the National League pennant—and the Cubs clinched the flag with a victory in the first game of a doubleheader in St. Louis. The win was Chicago's 20th straight in the stretch run, a streak they extended to 21 in the nightcap. Also, in the last month of the 2003 N.L. Central Division race, the clubs played two momentous series a week apart, the first eventually serving as the basis of a book about

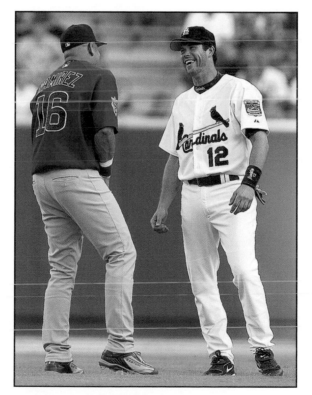

In the fierce battle of red vs. blue, friendships endure among the players—as Chicago's Aramis Ramirez and Cub-turned-Cardinal Mark Grudzielanek prove.

Cardinals manager Tony La Russa (the Cards won two of three games at Busch Stadium) and the second proving to be the key to the Cubs' run to the '03 divisional crown (Dusty Baker's team won four of five games at Wrigley Field).

Imagine the intensity of the rivalry and the attendant media glare should the two franchises engage in another heated fight for a championship. In view of the addition of the wild-card spot in the playoffs, it is possible for the Cardinals and Cubs to be matched in the National League Championship Series—with a berth in the World Series on the line.

As Harry Caray would say, "Holy cow!"

The
Unforgettables

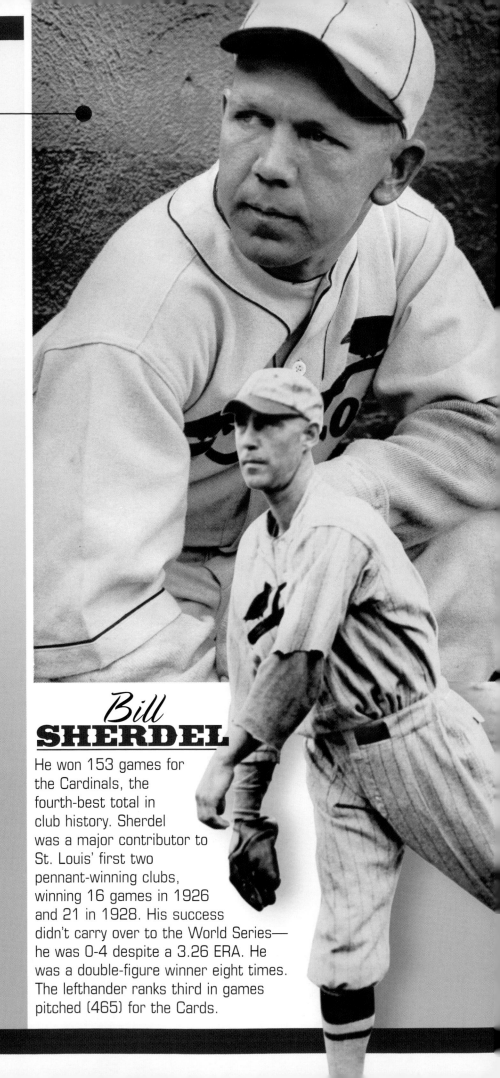

Bill
HALLAHAN

Nicknamed "Wild Bill," the lefthander led the league in walks three times—but also topped it in strikeouts twice. He was the N.L. starter and loser in the first All-Star Game (five walks in two-plus innings). He won 93 games in 10 seasons with the Cardinals, compiling 15-9 and 19-9 records in their pennant-winning seasons of 1930 and 1931. Hallahan pitched in seven games in four World Series, going 3-1 with a 1.36 ERA.

Bill
DOAK

He was known for throwing a spitball, but when he did it, the pitch was legal. Doak won 20 games in his first full year in the majors, 1914, and he compiled a National League-leading 1.72 ERA that season for the Cardinals. Seven years later, he again led the league in ERA. The righthander recorded 32 shutouts as a Cardinal, second on the all-time franchise list to Bob Gibson's 56.

Bill
SHERDEL

He won 153 games for the Cardinals, the fourth-best total in club history. Sherdel was a major contributor to St. Louis' first two pennant-winning clubs, winning 16 games in 1926 and 21 in 1928. His success didn't carry over to the World Series— he was 0-4 despite a 3.26 ERA. He was a double-figure winner eight times. The lefthander ranks third in games pitched (465) for the Cards.

Grover Cleveland
ALEXANDER

He spent only four of 20 major league seasons with the Cardinals but became a St. Louis legend because of his performance in the 1926 World Series (two victories and a dramatic relief outing in Game 7). Despite joining the Cards when he was 39 years old, Alexander went on to compile a 55-34 (.618) record for St. Louis and was a 21-game winner at age 40.

Bob
O'FARRELL

The catcher was named the National League's MVP in 1926, the Cardinals' first pennant-winning season. He ended the '26 World Series in stirring fashion, throwing out would-be basestealer Babe Ruth. His success and popularity helped earn O'Farrell the job as Cards player-manager the next season. St. Louis compiled a better record in 1927 under O'Farrell than in '26 under Rogers Hornsby, but the Cardinals lost out to the Pirates in a tight pennant race.

Branch
RICKEY

Although his playing and managerial records were not impressive, he became the architect of the Cardinals' winning ways. Rickey, who served the Cards in the front office from 1925 through 1942, was an astute judge of talent and a shrewd executive. Founder of the farm system, his skill in scouting and developing players was instrumental in the Cardinals' enormous success from 1926 through 1946, a period during which the Cards won nine pennants and six World Series.

Flint RHEM

He was one of the Cardinals' more spirited players in late-1920s, showing a penchant for getting into off-field trouble and talking his way out of it. His best season was 1926, when he tied for the National League lead in victories with 20. He had three stints with the Cards, winning 81 games in his 10 seasons with the club. He was a member of St. Louis' pennant-winning teams of '26, 1928, 1930 and 1931. He also was briefly with the Cardinals' 1934 champions.

Dizzy DEAN

Based on entertainment value alone, Dean was one of baseball's most memorable players. Braggadocio was part of his game, to be sure, but Dizzy also possessed a remarkable right arm. He personified the glorious Gas House Gang days of the 1930s, averaging 25 victories a year from 1933 through 1936. Dean also led the National League in strikeouts four consecutive years—he fanned 17 batters, then a modern major league record, in a 1933 game against the Cubs—and was named the league's MVP in 1934 after winning 30 games. He tossed seven shutouts in '34, a year in which he made 33 starts and worked 17 times out of the bullpen. His winning percentage as a Cardinal: .641.

Terry MOORE

Called "Captain" by his teammates for his leadership on and off the field, Moore never received the acclaim he deserved outside his own clubhouse. The center fielder had no peers defensively, and he was a consistent offensive player—as his .280 batting average over 11 seasons attests. A four-time All-Star Game participant, he played between Stan Musial and Enos Slaughter in the 1940s in what some consider one of the greatest outfields of all time. He lost three years in his prime because of military service.

Paul DEAN

He is known more as Dizzy's brother than for his own accomplishments—which is a slight to his ability. He won 19 games in each of his first two seasons, 1934 and 1935, but at age 22 "Daffy" saw his promising career short-circuited because of an arm injury. He underwent surgery for torn cartilage and never regained the velocity on his fastball. Dean won only eight more games as a Cardinal.

Pepper MARTIN

One of the stars of the Gas House Gang because of his fiery play, Martin was always sliding, diving and hustling. As a rookie outfielder, he helped lead the Cardinals to the 1931 pennant, then was a sensation in the World Series. He also was a key performer on the 1934 World Series championship team, this time as the Cards' third baseman. Martin had a career .418 batting average in World Series play. He topped the National League in stolen bases three times in one four-year span.

James "Rip" COLLINS

He enjoyed his greatest season in 1934, helping the Gas House Gang to the World Series title. He tied for the league lead in homers that year with 35 and wound up second in RBIs with 128. He also had a robust .333 batting average. In the Series against the Tigers, Collins hit .367. In six seasons with the Cardinals, he batted .307 and drove in 516 runs. One of many outstanding first basemen in Cards history, he was sandwiched between Jim Bottomley and Johnny Mize in the lineage.

Harry
WALKER

Walker delivered the hit that sent Enos Slaughter tearing around the bases for the winning run in Game 7 of the 1946 World Series. He lost two seasons in his prime because of military duty and had a regular spot in a crowded Cardinals outfield for only two years. Traded to the Phillies early in the 1947 season, he won the National League batting title that year. He served as Cards manager for most of 1955.

Del
RICE

He ranks second to Ted Simmons in games caught by a Cardinal. Only Rice and Simmons have logged more than 1,000 games behind the plate for the Cards. He spent 12 of his 17 big-league seasons with the Cardinals. Rice split time with Joe Garagiola early in his career, then settled in as a regular. Had 11 homers and 65 RBIs in 1952.

Joe
GARAGIOLA

He gained fame as a broadcaster in part by poking fun at his playing ability. In fact, he was a decent player. As a 20-year-old Cards rookie, Garagiola batted .316 in the 1946 World Series and had four hits in Game 4. Except for a stint in the minors in 1948, he was a Cardinal until 1951, when he was traded to the Pirates in a seven-player deal. He also played for the Cubs and Giants. Was 28 when his playing career ended.

Billy
SOUTHWORTH

As an outfielder, he helped the Cardinals to their first World Series title in 1926 after being acquired from the Giants. As a manager, he directed the Cards to pennants in 1942, 1943 and 1944. He's the only two-time World Series winner ('42, '44) among Cardinals managers. In the five seasons from 1941 through 1945, Southworth's Cardinals won 508 games. He also was manager of the 1948 pennant-winning Boston Braves.

Whitey
KUROWSKI

Kurowski overcame an arm injury to have a fine career. He was the regular third baseman on all four pennant-winning Cardinals teams of the 1940s. He hit a World Series-clinching home run in 1942, connecting for a two-run shot in the ninth inning of Game 5. Spent his entire nine-year major league career with the Cards. He batted .323 with 21 home runs and 102 RBIs in 1945. Hit 27 homers and drove in 104 runs in 1947. Kurowski played in three All-Star Games.

Marty
MARION

He was named the National League's MVP in 1944 because of his superb play at shortstop and his leadership skills. Marion earned the nickname Mr. Shortstop because of his defensive skills. A seven-time All-Star, ranks second to Ozzie Smith for most games at shortstop in his Cardinals' career. Spent all 13 years as a player in St. Louis, 11 with the Cardinals and two with the Browns.

Ted
WILKS

He had a sensational beginning to his Cardinals career, posting a 17-4 record as a starter/reliever in 1944 and then coming out of the bullpen in decisive Game 6 of the World Series to retire the Browns' final 11 batters. Wilks compiled a 12-0 mark over the 1946 and 1947 seasons, years in which he pitched almost exclusively in relief. He was 10-3 in '49. Wound up 51-20 as a Cardinal, 8-10 elsewhere.

Mort & Walker
COOPER

Mort was the pitcher and Walker the catcher, and the Cooper brothers were a force for the Cards. Mort was the N.L. MVP in 1942, going 22-7 with a league-low 1.78 ERA. Walker hit .281 that year. From '42 through '44, Mort was 65-22. Walker hit .318 in 1943 and .317 in 1944. Playing despite the death of their father earlier in the day, the Coopers formed the Cards' battery in Game 2 of the 1943 World Series. Mort won, 4-3.

George
KISSELL

The former minor league infielder never played in the majors, but he has been crucial in the development of Cardinals players since the 1940s. Most of his time has been spent as a manager or special instructor in the Cards' farm system. It was low-profile work but helped produce quality players at the big-league level. He also has been a Cardinals coach and a player-development coordinator.

Tom
ALSTON

Alston was the first black player to see action for the Cardinals, breaking into the big leagues with St. Louis on April 13, 1954—seven years after modern major league baseball had been integrated. The lanky first baseman, coming off a strong season in the Pacific Coast League, appeared in 66 games in '54, batting .246 with four homers. He saw brief duty with the Cardinals in each of the next three seasons.

Howie
POLLET

The lefthander won 21 games for St. Louis in 1946 and 20 in 1949. His final victory in '46 was an important one—it came in the opening game of a best-of-three pennant playoff with Brooklyn. He led the N.L. in earned-run average in 1943, went away to military duty the next two seasons and then won another ERA crown in his first season back. Pollet was 97-65 in nine seasons with the Cardinals. He later served as pitching coach for the Cards.

Solly
HEMUS

Hemus succeeded Marty Marion as the Cards' No. 1 shortstop in 1951. Played a key role in the team's greatest comeback—from an 11-0 deficit against the Giants in 1952. Hemus' eighth-inning homer tied the score and his two-run shot in the ninth provided the ultimate margin of victory in a 14-12 win. He managed the team for 2½ seasons, beginning in 1959.

Lindy
McDANIEL

The Cardinals' first star closer. He made 55 or more relief appearances for St. Louis from 1959 through 1962. In 1960, he compiled a 12-4 record, 2.09 ERA and 26 saves (not yet an official statistic). McDaniel spent 21 seasons in the majors; was 66-54 in his eight years with the Cards. He was the older brother of Von McDaniel, one of team's greatest pitching prospects. Von's career ended abruptly because of an arm injury.

Julian
JAVIER

Slick-fielding second baseman was a key player on the Cardinals' three pennant-winning teams in the 1960s. Javier was strong offensively in the Cards' championship season of 1967, hitting .281 with 14 homers and 64 runs batted in. He hit .346 for St. Louis in 15 World Series games. Stole 26 bases in 1962. Holds Cardinals career record for most games played at second base, outdistancing even Red Schoendienst. Ended his career with the Reds after 12 seasons as a Cardinal.

Curt FLOOD

Flood is best known for challenging the reserve clause after he was traded by St. Louis, but the center fielder was a gifted player, too. Flood, who came to the Cardinals at age 19 in a trade with the Reds, won seven consecutive Gold Gloves for St. Louis, and in one stretch played 226 games without an error. That flawless streak included the entire 1966 season, during which he handled 396 chances. Plus, Flood batted .300 or better six times, with highs of .335 in 1967 and .322 in 1961.

Orlando CEPEDA

Cepeda was a Cardinal for only two full seasons, but they were magical years. Obtained from the Giants in May 1966, "Cha-Cha" was named N.L. MVP award in 1967 after leading "El Birdos" to the pennant. He hit .325 with 25 homers and a league-high 111 RBIs for St. Louis, which went on to defeat Boston in the World Series. Cepeda fell off in '68 but still helped the Cards win back-to-back pennants for the first time since '43 and '44.

Curt SIMMONS

Signed in May 1960 after being released by the Phillies, he helped solidify the Cardinals' rotation. He was at his best in 1963 and 1964. In '63, he fashioned a 15-9 record and a 2.48 ERA. At age 35, he won 18 games for the '64 Cards, who went on to capture St.Louis' first World Series title in 18 years. Although best known because of his success with Philadelphia, Simmons was 69-58 for the Cards with a 3.25 ERA.

Larry JACKSON

Was a consistent, gritty pitcher for the Cardinals, posting victory totals of 15, 13, 14, 18, 14 and 16 from 1957 through 1962. He worked a National League-leading 282 innings in 1960, a year in which he made a league-high 38 starts. Traded to the Cubs after the '62 season, he won 24 games for Chicago in 1964—and lost 21 in 1965. He was a double-figure winner and loser in each of his final 11 major league seasons.

Roger
MARIS

Playing for the Yankees, he achieved what once seemed impossible—he broke Babe Ruth's single-season home run record. Yet Maris often said his most enjoyable years were spent with the Cardinals. Maris was a Cardinal in 1967 and 1968, years in which the outfielder was an integral part of pennant-winning teams. In St. Louis' seven-game victory over Boston in the '67 World Series, he hit .385 and drove in seven runs.

Mike
SHANNON

The St. Louis native was a Cardinal for nine seasons. He broke into the starting lineup in the Cards' championship season of 1964. St. Louis' No. 1 right fielder through 1966, he moved to third base when the Cardinals traded for Roger Maris. In the Cards' pennant-winning seasons of 1967 and 1968, he had RBI totals of 77 and 79. A kidney ailment forced his retirement. A crowd favorite as a player, he is highly popular as a Cards broadcaster.

Bill
WHITE

White hit 20 or more homers for St. Louis from 1961 through 1965 and topped the 100-RBI mark three straight seasons. In '61, he tied Ty Cobb's big-league record of 14 hits in two consecutive doubleheaders. Also excelled afield—he won six Gold Gloves in a row as the Cards' first baseman. Played in six All-Star Games as a member of the Cardinals. Traded to the Phillies after the 1965 season, he returned to the Cards briefly in 1969. Served as National League president from 1989 to 1994.

Tim
McCARVER

He was a rarity—a four-decade major leaguer. McCarver made his debut at age 17, getting into eight games with the 1959 Cardinals, and he bowed out with the Phillies in 1980. Played 12 of his 21 seasons for the Cardinals. Reliable and durable, he was a heady catcher and a tough hitter on St. Louis' standout 1964, 1967 and 1968 teams. He batted .478 in the '64 World Series and .333 in the '68 Series.

Ernie
BROGLIO

Broglio will live forever in Cardinals lore as the key man who went to the Cubs in the six-player 1964 trade that brought Lou Brock to St. Louis. The righthanded pitcher, soon beset by arm problems, proved a bust in Chicago and Brock evolved into a Hall of Famer for the Cards, but most people forget how good Broglio was as a Cardinal. In 1960, he won 21 games and had a 2.74 ERA; in 1963, he was 18-8.

Dal
MAXVILL

Never an offensive threat, Maxvill nevertheless was a good fit on successful Cardinals teams of his era. The shortstop was a Gold Glove winner in 1968 and made only 13 errors in both 1970 and 1971. He started all 21 games of the 1964, 1967 and 1968 World Series—in the '64 Series against the Yankees, Maxvill replaced the injured Julian Javier at second base. He served as general manager of the Cardinals from 1985 to 1994.

He spent only one season in St. Louis, 1970, but it was a memorable year. Obtained in the deal that sent Curt Flood and Tim McCarver to the Phillies, Allen hit 34 home runs, drove in 101 runs and started at first base for the National League in the All-Star Game. His home run total was the highest by a Cardinals player since Stan Musial hit 35 in 1954, and no Cardinal would hit more until Jack Clark connected for 35 in 1987.

Dick
ALLEN

Steve
CARLTON

Cardinals pitching coach Howie Pollet thought so much of teenager Carlton's potential in 1963 that he offered to pay his signing bonus. Six years later, the surefire star was 17-11 for the Cards with a 2.17 ERA and struck out a then-record 19 batters in one game (a contest he lost). Although most of his fame came after he left St. Louis—the left-hander was traded to the Phillies in February 1972 after a contract dispute—he was a 20-game winner for the Cardinals in 1971.

Bake
McBRIDE

Was the N.L. Rookie of the Year in 1974 after hitting .309 with 30 stolen bases. His steals total almost went unnoticed—Lou Brock had 118. The fleet McBride scored the winning run in the longest game in Cardinals history—a 25-inning marathon against the Mets in 1974. He led off the 25th with an infield single, raced to third on a botched pickoff attempt and scored when a throw to the plate was dropped. Hit .307 for the Cards over five seasons.

Joe TORRE

Enjoyed one of the finest seasons in Cardinals history in 1971, winning the N.L. batting title (.363) and leading the league with 137 RBIs and 230 hits. The league MVP also had 24 homers. Played third base in '71 but also was a first baseman and catcher as a Cardinal. Hit .308 for St. Louis over six seasons. Managed the team from 1990 to '95, then led the Yankees to four World Series titles in the next five years.

Bob FORSCH

Earned his spot in club history by becoming the only Cardinals pitcher to throw two no-hitters (vs. the Phillies in 1978, the Expos in 1983). He accomplished a lot more, though—he was a double-figure winner 10 times for the Cards and ranks third in franchise wins with 163. Was a 20-game winner in 1977. Forsch is third on the Cards' all-time strikeout list and fourth in games pitched.

Al HRABOSKY

The "Mad Hungarian" was entertaining even before throwing a pitch, psyching himself up near the mound and then storming to the rubber to face a hitter. Was at his dramatic best in a national-TV game on the night of May 9, 1977, when he struck out the Reds' George Foster, Johnny Bench and Bob Bailey with the bases full in the ninth inning of a tie game. Cards won in the 10th. Led the team in saves four straight years. In '75, he was 13-3 with a 1.67 ERA and shared the N.L. lead with 22 saves.

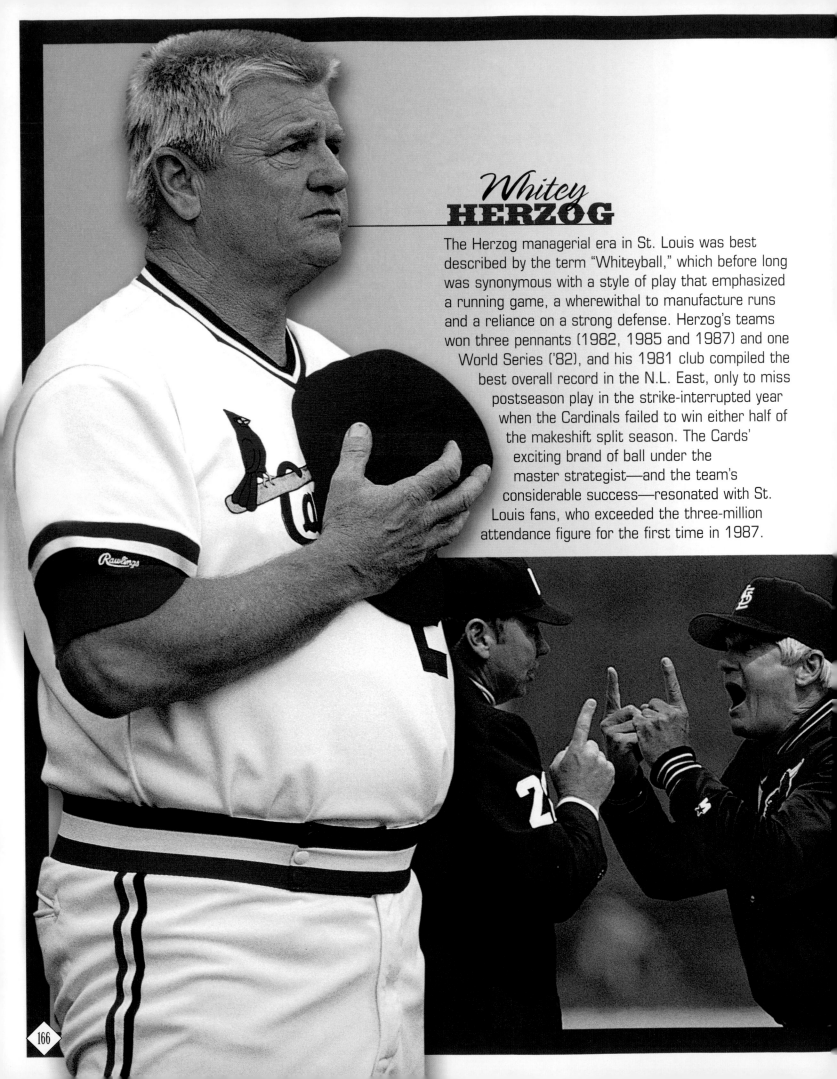

Whitey HERZOG

The Herzog managerial era in St. Louis was best described by the term "Whiteyball," which before long was synonymous with a style of play that emphasized a running game, a wherewithal to manufacture runs and a reliance on a strong defense. Herzog's teams won three pennants (1982, 1985 and 1987) and one World Series ('82), and his 1981 club compiled the best overall record in the N.L. East, only to miss postseason play in the strike-interrupted year when the Cardinals failed to win either half of the makeshift split season. The Cards' exciting brand of ball under the master strategist—and the team's considerable success—resonated with St. Louis fans, who exceeded the three-million attendance figure for the first time in 1987.

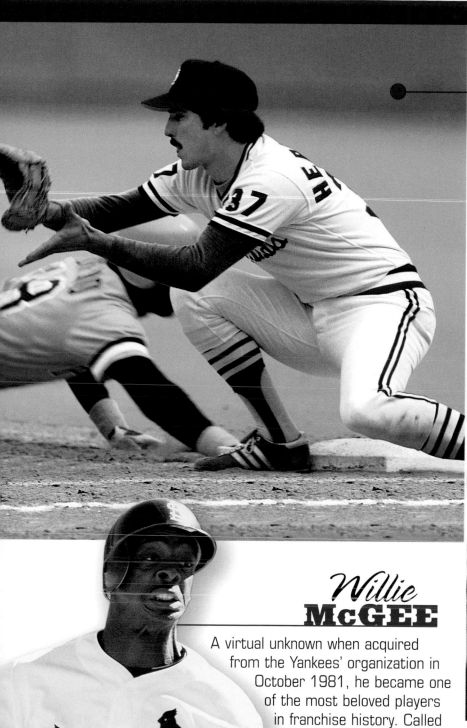

Keith
HERNANDEZ

One of the best defensive first basemen in the game's history, he won five consecutive Gold Gloves as a Cardinal and 11 in a row overall. Hernandez shared the 1979 MVP award with Pittsburgh's Willie Stargell after leading the league with a .344 average. That marked the first of three straight .300-plus years. He came up big in the '82 World Series win over Milwaukee, delivering a game-tying single in Game 7 and driving in eight runs overall.

Willie
McGEE

A virtual unknown when acquired from the Yankees' organization in October 1981, he became one of the most beloved players in franchise history. Called up from the minors in 1982, McGee helped the Cardinals to the pennant and had a sterling World Series that included a two-homer game and great defensive play. Was the league MVP in 1985; won N.L. batting title in '85 and 1990. Had two stints with the Cardinals totaling 13 seasons.

Garry
TEMPLETON

When shortstop Templeton was traded to San Diego for Ozzie Smith before the 1982 season, some thought the Padres wound up with the better all-around player. Templeton did possess great ability—he had two 200-hit years with the Cardinals, was the first switch hitter in the majors to get 100 hits from each side of the plate in one season and led the N.L. in triples three consecutive years. Whitey Herzog always raved about his sheer talent.

Todd WORRELL

He ranks third on the Cardinals' all-time saves list with 129, having recorded 101 saves over a three-year span (1986 through 1988). He was selected the National League's Rookie of the Year in '86 when he had a league-leading 36 saves and a 2.08 ERA. Had two saves in the 1987 World Series. Encountered major physical problems beginning in the late-1980s, but he rebounded with strong seasons (1995, 1996) with the Dodgers near the end of his career.

George HENDRICK

He was called "Silent George" because he wouldn't talk with the media. But he wasn't silent with his bat. Hendrick led the Cards in home runs four seasons in a row and in runs batted in five straight years (twice topping the 100-RBI mark). Got what proved to be the game-winning hit in Game 7 of the 1982 World Series. Helped the Cardinals even as he left—he was traded to Pittsburgh in the deal that brought John Tudor to St. Louis.

Vince COLEMAN

Was a key player on Cardinals teams of the mid-to-late 1980s. Stole 110 bases in 1985, a major league record for a rookie, en route to N.L. Rookie of the Year honors. Topped the 100-steal mark again in the next two years and led the N.L. six straight seasons. Was the victim of a freak accident before Game 4 of the 1985 NLCS, injuring his leg when run over by an automatic tarpaulin. Missed the rest of the '85 postseason.

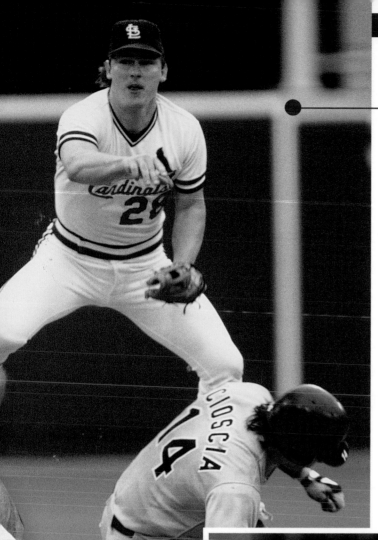

Tommy
HERR

The second baseman proved you don't have to be a power hitter to drive in runs—he had a 110-RBI season in 1985 despite hitting only eight home runs. Was a standout run-producer again in 1987, knocking in 83 runs during a season in which he had only two homers and 31 extra-base hits. Signed as an undrafted free agent, he made his Cardinals debut in 1979—on the night Lou Brock got his 3,000th hit. Had only 54 errors from 1981 through 1987. Was dealt to the Twins in 1988.

Joaquin
ANDUJAR

Andujar won 20 games in 1984 and 21 in 1985, becoming the first Cardinal to win 20 in consecutive seasons since Bob Gibson (1969, 1970). He was outstanding in 1982, too—as a 2.47 ERA attests. He often said that baseball was so unpredictable that it could be described in one word—"youneverknow." Won two games in the '82 World Series, including the clincher. He was ejected in Game 7 of the 1985 Series in Kansas City and traded to the Oakland A's six weeks later.

John
TUDOR

Holds Cardinals records for best career winning percentage (.705) and ERA (2.52). After a 1-7 start in 1985, Tudor won 20 of last 21 decisions. Led the league with 10 shutouts in '85 and finished with a 1.93 ERA. Never a hard thrower, he relied on location and an excellent changeup. Dealt to the Dodgers in 1988, he returned to the Cards in 1990 and went 12-4.

Darrell PORTER

He had been Whitey Herzog's catcher in Kansas City, and Herzog and the Cardinals lured the free agent to St. Louis in December 1980. Replacing the popular Ted Simmons, who had been traded, Porter did little to win over fans in 1981—but 1982 was a different story. He won MVP honors in both the '82 NLCS (.556 batting average) and the World Series (.286, five RBIs). Was a Cardinal for five seasons.

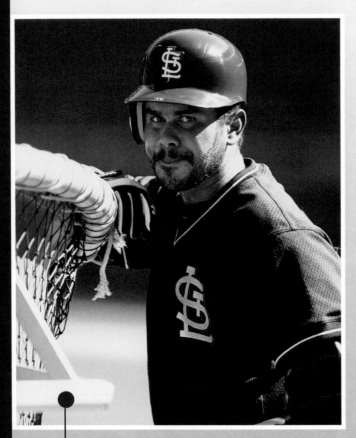

Jose OQUENDO

Super-sub who became a crowd favorite because of his ability to play anywhere during a 10-year Cardinals career. In 1988, he became the first N.L. player since 1918 to play all nine positions in one season. Enjoyed his best year in 1989 when, as the club's regular second baseman, he got 556 at-bats and hit .291. Set a franchise record for second basemen in 1990 with a .996 fielding percentage, committing only three errors in 681 chances.

Jack CLARK

He hit one of the most dramatic home runs in franchise history—a three-run shot in the ninth inning of Game 6 of the 1985 NLCS. The homer lifted the Cardinals into the World Series. Clark was the only real power source on the Cards' '85 and 1987 pennant-winners. Hit 35 homers in '87, most by a Cardinal in 33 years, and had 106 RBIs despite sitting out virtually the entire last month with an ankle injury. The Cards missed his bat in the World Series.

Terry
PENDLETON

He drove in 96 runs in 1987, helping the Cardinals win the pennant. In the heat of the race, he hit a tying two-run, two-out homer in the ninth inning of a key September game at Shea Stadium. The Cards beat the Mets in the 10th. Won two Gold Gloves as a Cardinal. Seven-year stint with St. Louis got off to a fast start when he hit .324 in 67 games in 1984.

Ray
LANKFORD

He had 20 or more home runs six times for the Cardinals. He hit 31 in both 1997 and 1998, driving in a total of 203 runs. Lankford was the first Cardinal with 30 homers in consecutive years since Stan Musial in 1954 and '55. Was traded to San Diego in the 2001 deal that brought pitcher Woody Williams to the Cardinals, but he returned in '04. Lankford is third on the Cards' all-time home run list with 228. Ranks No. 1 among Cardinals in homers hit at just-closed Busch Stadium with 122.

Fernando
TATIS

Major league baseball has been played for 130 seasons and only one man, the Cardinals' Tatis, has accomplished the feat of hitting two grand slams in the same inning. Tatis did it at Dodger Stadium on April 23, 1999, connecting for both bases-full home runs off Los Angeles starter Chan Ho Park in the third inning of a 12-5 Cards triumph. Acquired from Texas at the trading deadline in 1998, the third baseman finished the '99 season with 34 homers, 107 RBIs and a .298 batting average. Slowed by injuries the next year, Tatis was dealt to Montreal in December 2000 in the swap that brought Steve Kline to the Cardinals.

Mark

To some, McGwire is the man who brought back a sport that was left wheezing in the aftermath of the 1994 strike. McGwire's home runs went the farthest, and he hit them more often than anyone else.

To others, his accomplishments are tainted, considering the talk that his hulking body had

the help of chemicals, talk that grew louder when he didn't deny using steroids in front of a congressional panel in March 2005, about 3½ years after he had last swung a bat.

Though his legacy is clouded, the impact McGwire had on baseball during his days with the Cardinals is clear. He was baseball's No. 1 show, someone who made batting practice a

must-see event. He broke Roger Maris' 37-year-old home run record with No. 62 on September 8, 1998, then held off Sammy Sosa in a derby that captivated the nation. McGwire finished with 70 homers, four ahead of Sosa.

From the time Big Mac was acquired by the Cardinals on July 31, 1997—in a trade with the A's for pitchers T.J. Mathews, Eric Ludwick and Blake Stein—McGwire mania gripped St. Louis. Fans stood and roared for every at-bat by McGwire, who at the time of his acquisition was headed for free-agent status at season's end. Any concerns that he would be a short-timer were dashed when he signed a three-year deal with the team in September. That night, McGwire launched a 517-foot homer above the left field score-

board, a shot believed to be the longest in the 32-year history of Busch Stadium (a mark that would be broken twice the following season, both times by McGwire, of course).

If McGwire's arrival had an intoxicating effect on St. Louis, his record-breaking season of '98 had a dizzying one. He hit a grand slam on

opening day, then also homered in the next three games. Though he didn't keep up that homer-a-game pace, it often felt like he did. McGwire broke Maris' mark by hitting a 341-foot homer (his shortest of the season) down the left field line against the Cubs. Steve Trachsel was on the mound; Sosa looked on from right field. McGwire, though, couldn't put away Sosa for good until the season's final day, when he hit two against the Expos, No. 70 coming off Carl Pavano on McGwire's final swing of the season. Then, for an encore,

On September 8, 1998, with Sosa (58 homers and counting) looking on from right field, the record fell. McGwire's 62nd homer, ironically his shortest of the season at 341 feet, was a bullet down the left field line off Steve Trachsel. It set off a frenzied celebration.

McGwire hit 65 homers in 1999.

The McGwire that Cardinals fans saw in 2000 and 2001, however, was only a shell of his ball-crushing self of the late 1990s. Age and injuries, specifically a bum knee, prevented him from being a consistent contributor. In McGwire's last game in the big leagues, a loss to the Diamondbacks in Game 5 of the 2001 National League Division Series, Kerry Robinson (a slap hitter, of all things) pinch hit for him in the ninth inning. McGwire faxed in his retirement papers the following month.

The fans who crammed Busch to watch McGwire swing a bat also remember a softer side that complemented his power. They remember that he took less money to stay in St. Louis, that he gave millions to a foundation to help abused children, that he often had his son, Matt, serving as the batboy, hugging him as he crossed home plate.

Neatly summing up McGwire's place in Cardinals history isn't easy, but you can safely say he never will be forgotten.

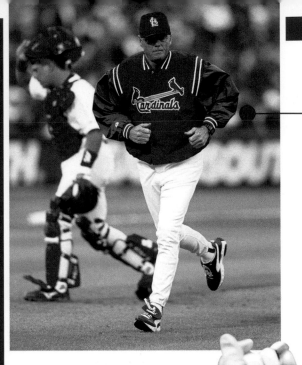

Dave
DUNCAN

"Dunc" has been Tony La Russa's pitching coach since 1983, serving as his most trusted confidant in Chicago, Oakland and St. Louis. Duncan spends games perched at the dugout railing, making notes in a thick binder that contains detailed statistical breakdowns and scouting reports. When one of Duncan's pitchers takes the mound, he has all of the information he needs to succeed. A big-league catcher for 11 seasons, Duncan has built a reputation for turning around veteran pitchers who have reached a career crossroad, a list that includes Andy Benes, Darryl Kile, Woody Williams and Chris Carpenter in St. Louis alone.

Edgar
RENTERIA

Renteria never was the star attraction with the Cardinals, but he held the lineup and clubhouse together with his consistency and approach. He sprayed line drives, drove balls into the gap, came through in the clutch and stole bases. He used his range and arm to shine in the field. From 1999-2004, Renteria was the best all-around shortstop in the N.L., someone who could be defined by Gold Glove ('02, '03) and Silver Slugger ('00, '02, '03) awards. Renteria's last at-bat with the Cardinals was a groundout that ended the '04 World Series in a sweep for the Red Sox, the team Renteria signed with two months later.

Darryl
KILE

Righthander Kile, whose death at age 33 near the midpoint of the 2002 season shocked Cardinal Nation and the baseball world, was a team leader who compiled a 41-24 record in a St. Louis uniform. Obtained from Colorado after the 1999 season, he won 20 games for the Cards in 2000. In 2001, he fashioned a 3.09 ERA on the way to posting a 16-11 mark. The fierce competitor was 5-4 after 14 starts in 2002 when he was found dead of heart problems in his Chicago hotel room.

Mike
MATHENY

Over his five years with the Cardinals, from 2000 through '04, Matheny batted .245. He never hit more than eight home runs or drove in more than 50 runs in a season. And for every time the catcher walked, he struck out 2.4 times. Those statistics hint that Matheny had a marginal impact on the team. Those statistics lie. Matheny won Gold Gloves in 2000, '03 and '04, and he committed only one error in his last two years with the Cardinals. Executives and scouts hail Matheny as one of the smartest players in baseball. He's as good as it gets when it comes to blocking pitches. Matheny had universal respect in the Cardinals' clubhouse because of his professionalism. He even helped show rookie Yadier Molina the way in 2004, even though Matheny knew Molina eventually would take his job.

Rick
ANKIEL

A cruel thing happened to Ankiel, the can't-miss kid. He missed. Badly. Ankiel reached the majors in his second pro year, 1999, and in 2000 he made 30 starts for St. Louis, using great velocity and a knee-buckling curve to strike out 194 in 175 innings. Tony La Russa surprisingly started Ankiel in Game 1 of the 2000 Division Series, and in $2\frac{2}{3}$ innings against Atlanta he walked six and fired five wild pitches. The meltdown continued in the NLCS. After six starts in '01, he was sent to Class AAA, where he had 17 walks and 12 wild pitches in $4\frac{1}{3}$ innings, and then to low-level ball. The lefty missed 2002 and much of '03 and '04 before deciding in March 2005 to give up pitching and try to make it as an outfielder.

Matt
MORRIS

Morris won 12 games as a rookie in 1997 and showed electric stuff. Injuries, though, began to take a toll. He missed the first half of '98 because of a shoulder injury and all of '99 following Tommy John surgery. He returned in 2000 and worked out of the bullpen. The shackles then were taken off, and Morris became a workhorse who won 39 games over the next two seasons. Lingering shoulder problems contributed to uneven seasons in 2003 and '04, but after offseason surgery, he started '05 as good as ever.

Steve KLINE

This off-center lefty might be best known for his grimy hat (and, occasionally, filthy mouth), or for flipping off his own manager from the bullpen in 2004, but Kline also should be remembered as a durable, dependable reliever for the Cardinals from 2001-04. He posted sub-2.00 ERAs in two of his four seasons and was particularly tough on lefthanders, which enabled Tony La Russa to use Kline and his sharp slider for key late-inning matchups. Kline pitched with emotion and flair, endearing him to many St. Louis fans.

Jim EDMONDS

Obtained from the Angels just before the 2000 season, center fielder Edmonds brought offensive punch and defensive panache to the Cards. He set career highs in 2000 with 42 home runs and 108 RBIs and also captured a Gold Glove. Edmonds topped his RBI mark in 2001 with 110 and then drove in 111 runs in 2004. He had another 42-homer season in '04, a year in which he won Game 6 of the NLCS with a 12th-inning homer and was awarded the seventh Gold Glove of his career. Known for his gliding, diving and expertly timed catches—including a gem in Game 7 of the '04 NLCS.

Jason ISRINGHAUSEN

Great closers have pitched in St. Louis, including Bruce Sutter, Todd Worrell and Lee Smith. That's hardly news to Isringhausen, a Brighton, Ill., native and lifelong Cardinals fan who came "home" as a free agent in December 2001. "Izzy" has upheld the tradition, particularly in '04 when he tied for the N.L. lead with 47 saves. While injuries have taken a toll, and he no longer flirts with 100 mph, Izzy still neutralizes hitters with fastballs, cutters and big curves. He often dances with danger, but at game's end a teammate usually flips the ball back to Izzy, another Cardinals win secured.

Chris CARPENTER

His face is boyish, his jaws usually working on a wad of bubble gum. Carpenter doesn't always look menacing. Then he steps on the mound. There, the righthander shoots his icy glare at hitters. The Cardinals signed Carpenter in December 2002 even though he was coming off shoulder surgery. His 2003 season was limited to eight minor league starts, but Carpenter became the ace of a balanced Cardinals staff in 2004. A biceps injury ended his season in September, causing him to miss the postseason, yet he came back even better in 2005 and won 21 games. Using his mix of power and precision, he improved his two-year Cardinals record to 36-10.

Scott ROLEN

When Rolen hits a home run, he puts his head down and sprints around the bases. No showmanship. When Rolen turns a scorching ground ball to his right into an easy out, experts wonder if anyone has played third base better. Rolen's no-nonsense approach, power and agility make him the consummate pro. Heisted from the Phillies in July 2002, Rolen hit .314 in 2004 with 34 homers and 124 RBIs (all career highs) despite missing much of September with a leg injury. His homer off Roger Clemens in Game 7 of the '04 NLCS sent the Cardinals to their first World Series since 1987. Injuries limited Rolen to 56 games in 2005.

The GREATEST MOMENTS

62

Roger Maris' major league record of 61 home runs in one season had stood for 37 years, and it really had not been threatened during that span. In the summer of 1998, however, Mark McGwire and the Cubs' Sammy Sosa came charging after Maris' mark, and when McGwire reached 62 on September 8 with a two-out, bases-empty homer in the fourth inning off the Cubs' Steve Trachsel at Busch Stadium, the baseball world erupted in celebration. Ironically, the home run—it was measured at 341 feet—was McGwire's shortest of the season.

1

McGwire Breaks Single-Season Home Run Record

— September 8, 1998 —

2
Enos Slaughter's Mad Dash

— October 15, 1946 —

The Cardinals and Red Sox were tied, 3-3, in Game 7 of the 1946 World Series when Enos Slaughter led off the bottom of the eighth inning with a single. He was still at first base two outs later when Harry Walker went to the plate for St. Louis. Walker hit a shot over shortstop Johnny Pesky's head into left-center. Slaughter took off, rounding second and heading for third. Center fielder Leon Culberson fielded the smash and threw to Pesky, who hesitated in making his relay to the plate—a throw that drew Red Sox catcher Roy Partee up the third-base line. Slaughter was home free. The Cards won, 4-3— Walker's hit was ruled a double—and were Series champions for the third time in five seasons.

MAD DASH

CLUBHOUSE CARDS: Slaughter
(opposite, far left) had plenty of help
in the '46 Series. Teammates also
playing key roles were (clockwise
from left) George "Red" Munger,
Whitey Kurowski and Joe Garagiola.

"GO CRAZY, FOLKS, GO CRAZY!"

As Ozzie Smith came to bat in the bottom of the ninth inning in Game 5 of the 1985 National League Championship Series against the Dodgers, a graphic flashed on the television screen. Smith, it noted, had never hit a home run batting lefthanded as a major leaguer. Not one in more than 3,000 at-bats. Shockingly, Smith then lined a pitch from Tom Niedenfuer over the right-field wall, giving the Cardinals a 3-2 victory and a three-games-to-two lead in the NLCS, moving St. Louis one win from a berth in the World Series.

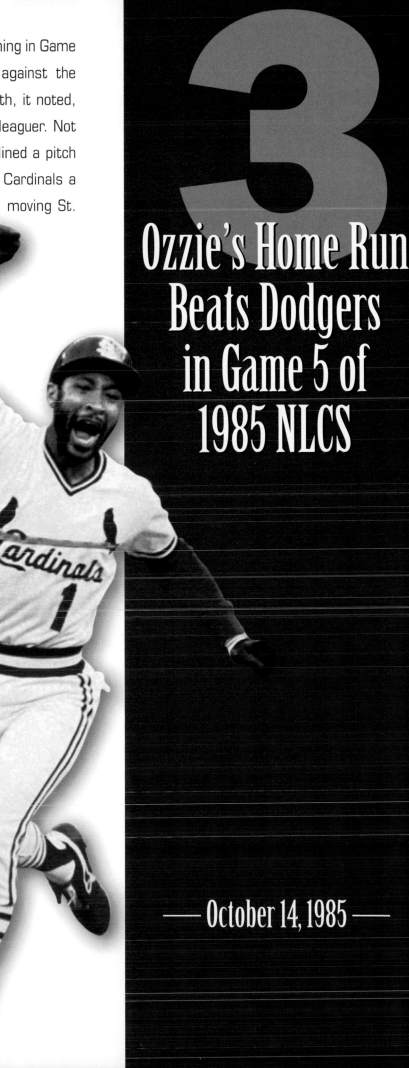

3

Ozzie's Home Run Beats Dodgers in Game 5 of 1985 NLCS

"Smith corks one into right, down the line, it may go. … Go crazy, folks, go crazy! It's a home run, and the Cardinals have won the game by the score of 3 to 2 on a home run by The Wizard. … Go crazy!"

—*Jack Buck*

— October 14, 1985 —

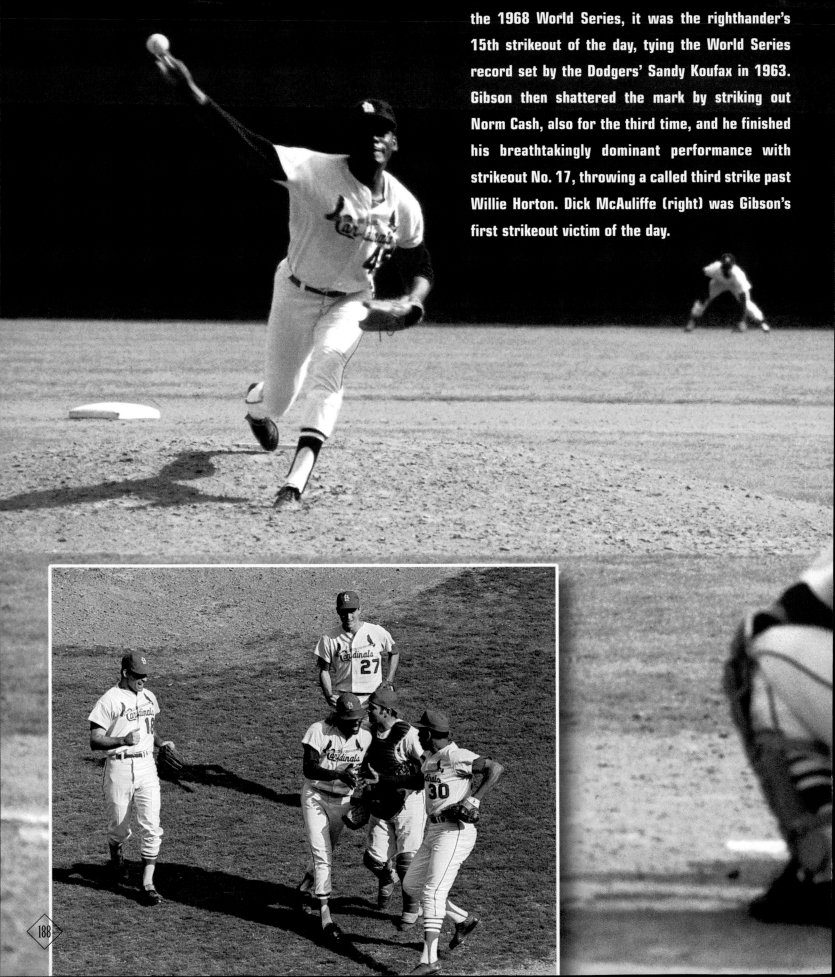

the 1968 World Series, it was the righthander's 15th strikeout of the day, tying the World Series record set by the Dodgers' Sandy Koufax in 1963. Gibson then shattered the mark by striking out Norm Cash, also for the third time, and he finished his breathtakingly dominant performance with strikeout No. 17, throwing a called third strike past Willie Horton. Dick McAuliffe (right) was Gibson's first strikeout victim of the day.

4

Gibson Strikes Out 17 in Game 1 of the 1968 World Series

— October 2, 1968 —

5

Alexander Strikes Out Tony Lazzeri in '26 World Series

Legend has it that when Grover Cleveland Alexander took over in relief with the bases loaded and two out in the seventh inning of Game 7 of the 1926 World Series, manager Rogers Hornsby told him there was nowhere to put the Yankees' Tony Lazzeri. Alexander's reply: "I reckon I'd better strike him out." That's exactly what he did, escaping the jam with the Cardinals' 3-2 lead intact. And Alexander, 39, who had pitched a complete-game victory the day before and, another legend goes, celebrated well into the night, made the lead stand up. The Cards were Series champions for the first time.

— October 10, 1926 —

> " I reckon I'd better strike him out. "

Game 6
Saturday, October 9, At New York

St. Louis	IP.	H.	R.	ER.	BB.	SO
Alexander (W)	9	8	2	2	2	6

Game 7
Sunday, October 10, At New York

St. Louis	IP.	H.	R.	ER.	BB.	SO.
Haines (W)	6⅔	8	2	2	5	2
Alexander	2⅓	0	0	0	1	1

6
Lou Brock Breaks Maury Wills' Stolen Base Record

— September 10, 1974 —

Lou Brock had been the game's best basestealer long before the 1974 season, but he had never stolen more than 74 bases in one year. Running wild at age 35 in the summer of '74, Brock was in hot pursuit of Maury Wills' major league record of 104 stolen bases in one season—he had 60 steals by the All-Star break. In a September 10 game against the Phillies at Busch Stadium, Brock tied Wills' record in the first inning and broke it in the seventh. When Brock made history, Dick Ruthven was the Phils' pitcher, Bob Boone their catcher and Larry Bowa their shortstop (below, attempting the tag). Cool Papa Bell (opposite), known for his speed and basestealing prowess for St. Louis' old Negro leagues team, presented the base to Brock. Lou finished the year with 118 steals.

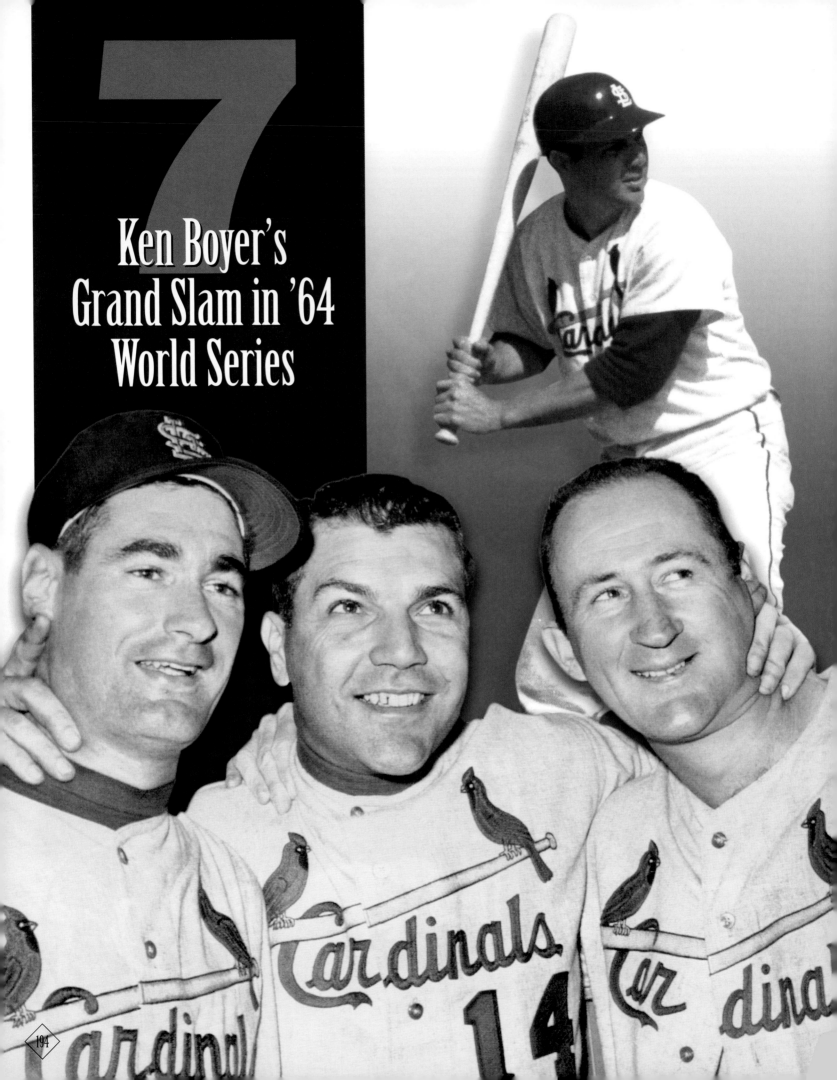

7

Ken Boyer's Grand Slam in '64 World Series

The Cardinals were facing a daunting task in the 1964 World Series. Down two games to one to the Yankees, they were trailing, 3-0, in the sixth inning of Game 4 at Yankee Stadium. Staring at the possibility of a three games-to-one deficit, the Cardinals filled the bases with one out against Al Downing. Ken Boyer, coming off what would be voted a Most Valuable Player season, came to the plate and rescued the Cards with a stadium-quieting grand slam. St. Louis held on to the 4-3 lead—the Cards got 8⅔ innings of scoreless relief that day from Roger Craig (opposite page, right) and Ron Taylor (opposite, far left)—and won the Series in seven games.

—— October 11, 1964 ——

GRAND

SLAM

8

Edmonds makes saving catch in the 2004 NLCS

One night after his 12th-inning home run won Game 6 of the 2004 NLCS, St. Louis' Jim Edmonds made a momentum-changing and what proved to be a pennant-saving catch in Game 7. With two Astros on base in the second inning and Houston already ahead, 1-0, center fielder Edmonds somehow ran down Brad Ausmus' deep drive—a smash that seemingly was about to go for extra bases and thrust the Astros into a three-run lead. The Cardinals, won, 5-2, and captured their 16th N.L. pennant.

— October 21, 2004 —

DECISIONS, DECISIONS: Dodgers manager Tommy Lasorda (2) made a bad one when he allowed Tom Niedenfuer (49) to face Jack Clark, who turned on the first pitch he saw (black and white photo, above).

With first base open, two outs, runners on second and third and the Dodgers leading, 5-4, in the ninth inning of Game 6 of the 1985 National League Championship Series, Los Angeles manager Tommy Lasorda elected to have Tom Niedenfuer pitch to cleanup hitter Jack Clark. Andy Van Slyke, who had collected one hit in the series, was on deck. The pennant was on the line, with the Cards holding a three-games-to-two edge in the NLCS. Clark hit the first pitch into the left-field bleachers at Dodger Stadium, propelling St. Louis into the World Series.

9

Jack Clark's Homer in Game 6 of 1985 NLCS

— October 16, 1985 —

3,00

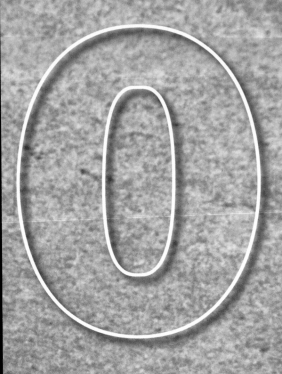

Cardinals manager Fred Hutchinson wanted Stan Musial to get his 3,000th career hit in St. Louis—so he left him out of the lineup for a May 13, 1958, game at Wrigley Field against the Cubs. Needing a pinch hitter in the sixth inning, though, Hutchinson called on Musial—and The Man came through with an RBI double off Moe Drabowsky for his milestone hit. Musial became only the eighth player in major league history to attain 3,000 hits.

10

Musial Collects 3,000th Hit

— May 13, 1958 —

The GREATEST PERFORMANCES

BOB GIBSON

1.12 ERA

To call Bob Gibson's 1968 season the greatest performance in Cardinals history is not enough. His dazzling numbers add up to one of the finest years ever recorded by a pitcher in the game's history. Start with a minuscule earned-run average of 1.12, still a major league record for 300 or more innings pitched. Then consider a 22-9 won-lost record that featured 13 shutouts (the highest total in the majors since 1916)—and 28 complete games in 34 starts. Plus, Gibson struck out a league-high 268 batters and walked only 62 in 304⅔ innings.

After batting .397 in 1921 and .401 in 1922, Rogers Hornsby "slumped" to a .384 mark in 1923. The man acknowledged as the game's greatest righthanded hitter responded with an astonishing .424 average in 1924, a post-1900 major league high. He also led the league that year in runs scored (121), hits (227), doubles (43), walks (89) and slugging percentage (.696). The No. 2 man in the batting race wound up 49 points behind Hornsby, and the runner-up in slugging percentage finished at .552. Hornsby was amid a remarkable tear—from 1921 through 1925, he batted .402.

24

ROGERS HORNSBY

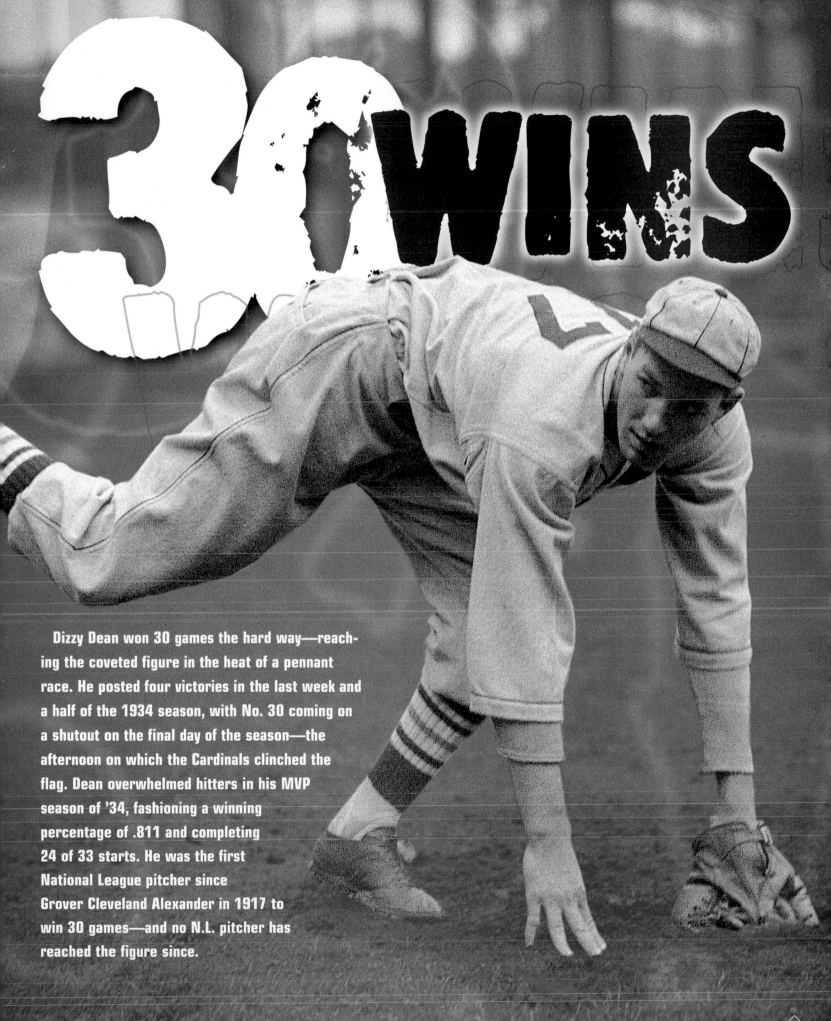

30 WINS

Dizzy Dean won 30 games the hard way—reaching the coveted figure in the heat of a pennant race. He posted four victories in the last week and a half of the 1934 season, with No. 30 coming on a shutout on the final day of the season—the afternoon on which the Cardinals clinched the flag. Dean overwhelmed hitters in his MVP season of '34, fashioning a winning percentage of .811 and completing 24 of 33 starts. He was the first National League pitcher since Grover Cleveland Alexander in 1917 to win 30 games—and no N.L. pitcher has reached the figure since.

WORLD

Coming back from a broken leg is one thing. Coming back the way Bob Gibson did in the 1967 World Series is quite another. Sidelined eight weeks after being struck by a smash off the bat of Pittsburgh's Roberto Clemente in mid-July, Gibson rounded into shape with five starts in the final weeks of the regular season. He appeared primed for the Series against Boston (left, with Red Sox Game 1 starter Jose Santiago)— and that is an understatement. Gibson won the opener, 2-1, striking out 10 batters; he threw a five-hit shutout in Game 4; and in Game 7, he was a 7-2 winner, again fanned 10 and hit a home run. Three victories, three complete games, 14 hits allowed and a 1.00 ERA.

BOB GIBSON

SERIES

HOME RUNS
IN A

On May 2, 1954, in St. Louis against the New York Giants, Stan Musial did what no one had ever done—he hit five home runs in a doubleheader. After connecting for three homers in the opener— two off Johnny Antonelli and one against Jim Hearn—Musial delivered an encore of two homers, both off Hoyt Wilhelm. He was retired on another long drive, a 410-foot smash that center fielder Willie Mays ran down in the nightcap. Musial was 4-for-4 in the first game and 6-for-8 overall, and he finished the day with nine RBIs. Somehow, the Cards managed only a split of the two games.

DOUBLEHEADER

6 ALBERT PUJOLS

5 SEASONS OF GREATNESS

The label of greatness most often is bestowed upon a player because of a superior performance over an extended time. That label already fits first baseman Albert Pujols despite the St. Louis slugger's mere five years in the major leagues. And rightly so. Pujols has been a hitting sensation since making the Cardinals' roster out of spring training in 2001. He won unanimous N.L. Rookie of the Year honors in '01, a year in which he set a league rookie record with 130 RBIs. In 2003, Pujols captured the N.L. batting championship, reeled off a 30-game hitting streak and was named the SPORTING NEWS Major League Player of the Year; in 2004, he bashed a career-high 46 home runs. Then, in 2005, he became the first player in big-league history to reach the 30-homer plateau in each of his first five seasons and only the fourth major leaguer to begin his career with five consecutive 100-RBI years. His eye-popping career numbers after five seasons in the majors: 982 hits, 201 homers, 621 RBIs and a .332 batting average.

ALBERT PUJOLS

HOME 4 IN 1

Mark Whiten was playing in only his fourth major league season and had just 38 career home runs entering the Cardinals' September 7, 1993, double-header in Cincinnati. After going 0-for-4 with one RBI in the opener, Whiten went on an unfathomable spree in the second game. He became the 12th player in

big-league history to hit four home runs in one game and only the second to drive in 12 runs in a single contest. He blasted a grand slam off Larry Luebbers in the first inning, three-run homers against Mike Anderson in the sixth and seventh and a two-run homer off Rob Dibble in the ninth.

MARK WHITEN

RUNS
GAME

8

JIM BOTTOMLEY

12 RBIs IN

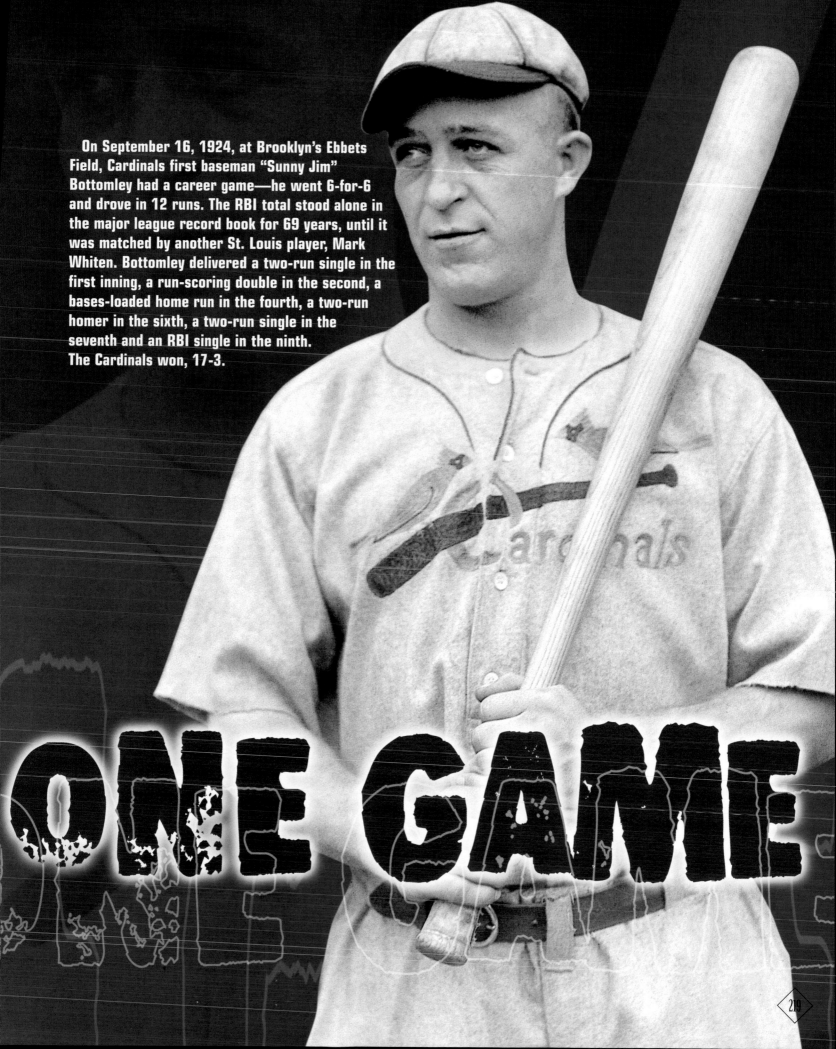

On September 16, 1924, at Brooklyn's Ebbets Field, Cardinals first baseman "Sunny Jim" Bottomley had a career game—he went 6-for-6 and drove in 12 runs. The RBI total stood alone in the major league record book for 69 years, until it was matched by another St. Louis player, Mark Whiten. Bottomley delivered a two-run single in the first inning, a run-scoring double in the second, a bases-loaded home run in the fourth, a two-run homer in the sixth, a two-run single in the seventh and an RBI single in the ninth. The Cardinals won, 17-3.

ONE GAME

PEPPER MARTIN

'31 WORLD SERIES

It was a dramatic way for Pepper Martin to cap his first season of full-time duty in the major leagues. Taking center stage in the Cardinals' seven-game World Series victory over the Philadelphia Athletics in 1931, center fielder Martin batted .500, drove in five runs, scored five times and stole five bases. The "Wild Horse of the Osage," who collected 12 hits in his first 18 at-bats in the '31 Series, went 3-for-4 in both Game 1 and Game 5 (a contest in which he hit a two-run homer off Waite Hoyt and knocked in four runs).

SHUTOUTS

5

10

Cardinals rookie lefthander Larry Jaster started five games against the National League champion Los Angeles Dodgers in 1966—and he shut out the Dodgers all five times. In an odd twist, Jaster spent six weeks in the minors between his first and second shutouts of Los Angeles. The Dodgers never even managed an extra-base hit off Jaster, who allowed 24 singles over 45 innings and spun his shutouts on April 25, July 3, July 29, August 19 and September 28. Jaster was 6-5 against the rest of the league with no shutouts. He wound up pitching four seasons with the Cards, going 32-25.

LARRY JASTER

223

The
CARDINALS
CHRONOLOGY

CARDINALS
CHRONOLOGY

1892

Offseason—The National League adds four cities—including St. Louis—that had teams in the American Association, a major league from 1882 through 1991. St. Louis' A.A. franchise (the Browns), owned by Chris Von der Ahe, has a virtually new roster and a new manager (Von der Ahe himself) as it prepares for competition in the N.L. (St. Louis previously fielded N.L. teams in 1876-77 and 1885-86.)

Apr. 12—The Cardinals franchise—known first as the Browns, later as the Perfectos and then as the Cardinals—makes its N.L. League debut with a 14-10 loss to Chicago at Sportsman's Park, located at Grand Avenue and Dodier Street.

Apr. 17—The Browns lose, 5-1, to Cincinnati in the first National League game played on a Sunday. The club had many Sunday games in the A.A. and was allowed to keep the tradition as part of its agreement to enter the N.L.

Oct. 13—The Browns end their inaugural N.L. season. The season is split, and the Browns go 31-42 in the first half and 25-52 in the second. The overall record of 56-94 places them 11th in the 12-team league. Five managers are employed by the Browns. A bright spot: righthanded pitcher Kid Gleason, who becomes the franchise's first 20-game winner (20-24).

1893

March 7—In an important rule change, the N.L. eliminates the pitching box and adds a pitcher's rubber five feet behind the previous back line of the box, establishing the modern pitching distance of 60 feet, six inches.

Apr. 27—The Browns open the season at their new ballpark, to be known as Robison Field, at the corner of Natural Bridge and Vandeventer avenues. Bill Watkins is the new manager as St. Louis defeats Louisville, 4-2.

Sept. 30—The Browns close the season with a doubleheader sweep of league champion Boston, with rookie catcher Duff Cooley going 6-for-6 in the second game, a 16-4 St. Louis romp. The weather is terrible and the attendance is low, about 1,500. Between games of the doubleheader a ceremony is held at which Joe Quinn, Charlie Frank and Ted Breitenstein of the Browns are given medals by the SPORTING NEWS, a St. Louis-based weekly magazine, for finishing first, second and third in a TSN poll for the most popular baseball player in America. Quinn celebrates by collecting eight hits in the doubleheader, the first player to accomplish the feat. The Browns lead the league with a 4.06 ERA but finish in 10th place at 57-75, chiefly because they rank 11th in scoring and allow more than two unearned runs per game.

1894

May 10—The Browns, with a new manager in George Miller, slug six home runs in a game but lose at Cincinnati, 18-9. The Reds parlay nine singles, a walk, a hit batsman and two errors to score 11 runs in one inning. Frank Shugart and St. Louis native Heinie Peitz hit two homers apiece for the Browns.

Sept. 30—The Browns sweep a doubleheader at home against Washington and finish in ninth place at 56-76, 35 games behind N.L. champion Baltimore. Roger Connor, who finishes the season in second place on the all-time home run list, finds triples to his liking, finishing the year with a team-high 25. Connor had been acquired from New York early in the season.

1895

June 1—Connor goes 6-for-6 and the Browns rap out a team-record 30 hits in a victory over New York.

June 3—Connor hits the 122nd homer of his career to pass Harry Stovey and become major league baseball's all-time home run leader. The homer, Connor's fourth of the season, accounts for the Browns' only two runs in a 5-2 loss to Brooklyn.

Aug. 16—Tommy Dowd becomes the first player in the history of the N.L. franchise to hit for the cycle.

Sept. 28—Under four managers, one of them team owner **Von der Ahe**, the Browns go 39-92 and finish in 11th place, 48½ games behind pennant-inning Baltimore and just four games ahead of last-place Louisville.

VON DER AHE

1896

January—The Browns' best pitcher, **Breitenstein**, angers Von der Ahe by performing in a play called *The Derby Winner* in a Baltimore theater. The time that Breitenstein spends on his acting career,

the Browns owner feels, could be better spent getting in shape for the coming season. Breitenstein disagrees and takes his case before the National Board of Arbitration, claiming the St. Louis club had not reserved him by the March 1 deadline. While Breitenstein holds out, Von der Ahe orders his ace lefty to report by April 1 "in proper condition to play ball." Breitenstein pitches the entire 1896 season in St. Louis (and accounts for 18 of the team's 40 wins) but is sold by a disgruntled Von der Ahe to the Cincinnati Reds for a reported $10,000 after the season.

Sept. 3—Boston pulverizes the Browns, 28-7, as Billy Hamilton, Jimmy Collins and Fred Tenney each collect five hits.

Sept. 26—The Browns go through five managers and finish 40-90, compiling a 13-43 record on the road. They wind up 50½ games behind first-place Baltimore and just 2½ games ahead of last-place Louisville. Three St. Louis pitchers lose 24 or more games—Breitenstein (26), Bill Hart (a league-worst 29) and Red Donahue (24). Connor hits 11 homers, fourth-best figure in the league, in the next-to-last season of his illustrious major league career.

1897

May 23—With his team mired in last place and desperate for fans, Von der Ahe opens a "shoot the chutes" waterslide at his ballpark. The waterslide quickly becomes more popular than the team but is removed after the season.

Sept. 2—The Browns prevail in 10 innings at Baltimore, 4-3, behind rookie pitcher Willie Sudhoff. They don't win again until Sept. 27.

Sept. 26—The visiting Cincinnati Reds sweep a doubleheader from the Browns by scores of 10-4 and 8-6. The outcome shocks no one as the Browns enter the twin bill riding a 16-game losing streak and a 21-game futility skein against the Reds, a team they last beat in 1895.

Oct. 3—The Browns end a miserable season with a doubleheader split against Chicago. In the first game, 45-year-old **Cap Anson** belts two homers against St. Louis in his final day as a major league player. The Browns become just the second major league team to lose 100 games, going 29-102 and finishing 63½ games out of first place, 23½ games behind 11th-place Louisville.

ANSON

1898

Apr. 16—During a game against the Chicago Orphans, a fire breaks out at the Browns' park and burns down most of the facility and Von der Ahe's saloon. About 100 people are injured, several seriously, and Von der Ahe, who already is in financial trouble, is slapped with several lawsuits. In addition, the money Von der Ahe has to spend to rebuild the park leaves him with little cash to pay his bills. The incident leads to his eventual departure as Browns owner.

Apr. 17—After nearly 150 carpenters (and many Browns players) spend much of the previous night working at the burned-out ballpark to make it playable again, the Browns are clobbered by the Orphans, 14-1. Chicago scores 10 runs in the fourth inning and the Browns, many weary from helping to rebuild the park the night before, commit 11 errors. Typical is the play of Lou Bierbauer, who plays so poorly at second base that he is yanked by disgruntled first-year manager Tim Hurst, who doesn't seem to understand why his players are tired.

Oct. 15—The Browns finish 63½ games out of first place for the second consecutive season. At 39-111, St. Louis sets a major league record for losses. Hurst never again manages in the major leagues.

1899

March 14—Von der Ahe's reign as Browns owner ends when the club, after some negotiations, is awarded on April 3 to Frank de Haas Robison and **Matthew Stanley Robison**. The Robisons also own the Cleveland Spiders and move Cleveland's best players, including **Cy Young**, Jesse Burkett and Bobby Wallace, over to the Browns.

YOUNG

Apr. 15—St. Louis opens a season of considerable promise with a 10-1 romp over Cleveland. Red replaces brown as the coloring on the team's uniforms and the team nickname is now the Perfectos.

Aug. 1—With St. Louis and Boston tied, 7-7, in the 14th inning, Perfectos pitcher Jack Powell hits a ball over the head of center fielder Billy Hamilton for a game-winning, inside-the-park homer.

Oct. 15—A season that opened with much excitement ends with St. Louis posting its first winning season (84-67). Burkett becomes the first player in club history to have a 200-hit season (228). After the season, the Robisons take up a suggestion by sports reporter William McHale to rename the team the Cardinals.

1900

March 8—The N.L. shrinks from 12 to eight teams and players from the four eliminated teams (Baltimore, Cleveland, Louisville and Washington) are sold to the remaining clubs. The Cardinals purchase third baseman-manager **John McGraw**, catcher Wilbert Robinson and infielder Bill Keister from Baltimore. After a prolonged contract holdout, McGraw and Robinson make their Cardinals debuts on May 12.

May 12—McGraw, leading off and playing third base, reaches base in four of his five at-bats and drives in a run in his first game with St. Louis. But he makes an error in the ninth inning that contributes to a 5-4 loss to the visiting Brooklyn Superbas, who score three runs in the final frame. Robinson goes 3-for-4 at the plate, smashing a ball that hits a flag pole on the left field line and bounces back onto the field for a double.

Oct. 14—The Cardinals finish 65-75 and slip into a tie for fifth place, 19 games behind first-place Brooklyn. Young goes 20-18 in his final season with the club and allows a team-record 337 hits. McGraw, Robinson and Young leave the Cardinals at the end of the season to join Ban Johnson's newly formed American League.

1901

July 8—Pandemonium rules as St. Louis fans take umbrage at two calls by umpire Hank O'Day and take aim on the arbiter following a 7-6 loss to Brooklyn. In the eighth inning, with the Cardinals leading, 4-3, O'Day calls two Brooklyn baserunners safe on the same play when they appear to be out. One of the runners, Cozy Dolan, runs five to 10 feet into the infield to avoid being tagged out after hitting a weak grounder to first baseman Dan McGann. By rule, he should have been out. The second runner, Tom Daly, appears clearly to be tagged out by Cardinals catcher Jack Ryan as he tries to score from third base. But both are ruled safe. The St. Louis players, faced with a one-out, two-on jam and a tie game instead of an inning-ending double play, argue vehemently with O'Day,

but to no avail. Some fans toss beer bottles toward O'Day and others jump from the bleacher seats, hoping to get their hands on the beleaguered ump. When order is finally restored and the game is resumed, both runners eventually score to give the Superbas the lead. Police have to escort O'Day from the field.

July 15—Giants rookie Christy Mathewson pitches a 5-0 no-hitter against the Cardinals in St. Louis.

Sept. 19—No games are played out of respect for President William McKinley, whose funeral is held this day. McKinley, who was shot on September 6, died on September 14.

Oct. 6—The Cardinals improve to 76-64 and finish fourth, 14½ games behind N.L. champion Pittsburgh. Burkett hits .376 to win his third and final batting title.

1902

May 6—The Robisons lose a lawsuit that attempts to block Burkett, Wallace and pitcher Jack Harper from joining St. Louis' American League club, the Browns.

June 3—Pitcher **Mike O'Neill** hits the first pinch-hit grand slam in major league history off Boston's Togie Pittinger in an 11-9 St. Louis triumph. It is an inside-the-park homer that scores his brother Jack.

Aug. 17—The Cardinals and Brooklyn Superbas play an 18-inning, 7-7 deadlock in a game called because of darkness. Rookie righthander Clarence "Cupid" Currie pitches 16 innings out of the bullpen for St. Louis.

Oct. 5—The Cardinals are swept at home in a double-header against Chicago and finish the season in sixth place at 56-78, 44½ games behind N.L. champ Pittsburgh.

O'NEILL

1903

July 22—The Cardinals win their fourth consecutive game in their final at-bat, this time 8-7 over Cincinnati. After the Reds score two runs in the top of the ninth to take a 7-5 lead, outfielder Homer Smoot connects for a three-run homer with two out in the bottom of the inning to give St. Louis the victory. The Cardinals' starter is rookie righthander **Mordecai Brown**, a three-fingered Indiana coal miner who allows nine hits over four innings.

Sept. 27—The Cardinals split a season-ending doubleheader with Philadelphia and finish in last place at 43-94, 46½ games behind first-place Pittsburgh.

Dec. 12—The Cardinals trade Brown, coming off a 9-13 debut season, and catcher Jack O'Neill to the Cubs for catcher Larry McLean and pitcher Jack Taylor. It's a terrible trade for the Cardinals. Brown will go on to a Hall of Fame career with Chicago, recording six consecutive 20-win seasons (1906-11).

1904

Feb. 1—The Cardinals purchase veteran first baseman Jake Beckley from the Cincinnati Reds. Beckley, who has 2,501 career hits, will add just 429 to that total in his final four big-league seasons in St. Louis.

June 16—Mathewson, a loser against St. Louis on May 4, beats the Cardinals for the first of six times this season and what will become 24 straight times overall. Of course, Mathewson beats more teams than just St. Louis in 1904—the Giants' star righthander goes 33-12 and leads the league in strikeouts.

Oct. 4—Taylor pitches his 39th consecutive complete game, an N.L. single-season record. It comes one day after Mathewson strikes out a record 16 Cardinals in a 3-1 Giants victory.

Oct. 9—The Cardinals improve by 32 victories in the first season of the 154-game schedule but finish in fifth place at 75-79, 31½ games behind the pennant-winning New York Giants.

1905

Feb. 15—Taylor, who was accused of throwing games by Cubs owner James Hart, is acquitted by the league office but fined $300 for bad conduct.

May 29—Five weeks before he is traded to the Pirates, Cardinals infielder Dave Brain hits three triples in a game against his future Pittsburgh teammates.

Oct. 8—The Cardinals lose both ends of a doubleheader at Chicago and finish in sixth place at 58-96, 47½ games behind the first-place Giants.

Oct. 15—The Browns sweep a doubleheader against the Cardinals to win the "City Series." The scores are 7-6 and 3-0, with the second game being called because of darkness after six innings. Harry Howell wins both games for the Browns; Taylor loses both for the Cardinals. Future Hall of Famer Bill Klem umpires both games, which are played one day after the end of a five-game World Series between the New York Giants and Philadelphia Athletics.

1906

Apr. 28—The Pirates beat the Cardinals, 10-1, in a game highlighted by a steal of home by Pittsburgh player-manager Fred Clarke.

June 9—The N.L.'s worst team, the Boston Beaneaters, snaps a 19-game losing streak by defeating the Cardinals.

July 20—Brooklyn's Mal Eason no-hits the Cardinals.

August 13—Taylor, after being traded to the Cubs on July 1, is knocked out in the third inning of a game against Brooklyn, ending a string of 187 complete games and 15 relief appearances in which he finishes each game. The streak began in 1901 during Taylor's first stint with the Cubs.

Oct. 7—The Cardinals finish seventh at 52-98, 63 games behind first-place Chicago and just 2½ games ahead of last-place Boston. No St. Louis pitcher wins more than nine games, and Beckley leads the team with 44 RBIs. As a team, the Cardinals hit a franchise-low 10 home runs.

1907

May 20—The Cardinals beat the Giants, 6-4, at the Polo Grounds to end New York's 17-game winning streak.

Aug. 11—The Cardinals complete a five-game sweep of Boston by winning two games in St. Louis, 5-4 and 4-0. A crowd of 12,000—the largest of the season—looks on as righthander Stoney McGlynn and lefty Ed Karger befuddle the Boston club. In the second game, which is limited to seven innings by mutual agreement of the teams, Karger retires all 21 batters he faces. He is so dominant that had the game gone the normal distance, Karger might well have pitched the only nine-inning perfect game in Cardinals history.

Sept. 1—The Cardinals rally from a 2-0 ninth-inning deficit at Chicago by scoring seven runs against Cubs righthander Ed Reulbach for a 7-2 win. What makes the victory so stunning is that the Cardinals are a last-place team and Reulbach is a star who will finish the season with a 17-4 record and a 1.69 ERA.

Sept. 30—The Cardinals set a major league record with three steals of home in a game against Boston. Ed Konetchy performs the feat twice and fellow rookie Joe Delahanty, younger brother of Hall of Famer-to-be Ed, does it once.

Oct. 6—The Cardinals split a doubleheader at home against the Cubs and finish in last place at 52-101. The Cards hit just .232 for the season and McGlynn loses a team-record 25 games.

1908

Apr. 20—Despite allowing just one hit—and a disputed one at that—to the visiting Chicago Cubs, Cardinals righthander Bugs Raymond loses his first start of the season, 2-0. Raymond's teammates offer him little support, getting six hits off Cubs starter Carl Lundgren and committing five errors. It would have been six errors had a grounder by Harry Steinfeldt that went through the legs of shortstop Patsy O'Rourke—the only "hit" Raymond allows—been ruled correctly.

Sept. 15—**Mathewson** beats the Cardinals for the 24th consecutive time, setting a record for dominance against an opponent.

Sept. 25—Frank de Haas Robison dies of a stroke at age 54 in Cleveland.

Oct. 4—A miserable season ends with a 5-1 loss at Cincinnati. The Cardinals, who lose a team-record 27 games in September, drop into the N.L. cellar at 49-105 and finish 50 games behind the first-place Cubs. St. Louis is shut out 33 times and commits 93 more errors than the league's next-worst fielding team. Raymond loses 25 games, 11 by shutout.

Dec. 12—The Cards acquire catcher **Roger Bresnahan** from the Giants for three players and give him a four-year deal to become player-manager.

BRESNAHAN

1909

May 24—After 24 straight losses to Mathewson, the Cardinals finally beat the future Hall of Famer, 3-1, in New York. Mathewson pitches well, but Cardinals lefty Johnny Lush is at least his equal and Giants fielders are erratic. All three St. Louis runs are unearned. The game is Bresnahan's first in New York after last December's trade.

July 3—The Cardinals are swept in a doubleheader at Cincinnati and tie a National League record (since 1900) with 11 errors in the second game.

July 24—Brooklyn lefthander George "Nap" Rucker strikes out 16 Cardinals in a 1-0 win.

Aug. 3—Former Cardinals manager Tim Hurst, now an A.L. umpire, has to be escorted out of Philadelphia's Shibe Park under police protection following an altercation with A's star Eddie Collins. Hurst spits in Collins' face after incurring his wrath—Collins had been called out by Hurst on a play at second base. A.L. president Ban Johnson fires Hurst.

Oct. 6—The Cardinals go 54-98 in their first season under Bresnahan and finish seventh, 56 games behind first-place Pittsburgh. Fred Beebe, 15-21, becomes the team's fourth 20-game loser in five years.

1910

May 4—**William Howard Taft**, who in April had become the first U.S. president to throw out the ceremonial first pitch on opening day, takes in a Cardinals game in St. Louis. After seeing the Cards jump to a big lead against the Reds (St. Louis wins, 12-3), he heads to Sportsman's Park to watch the Browns play the Cleveland Indians. The Browns and Indians lock up in a 3-3 duel that is called after 14 innings because of darkness.

June 1—Cardinals second baseman Miller Huggins comes to the plate six times in a game and doesn't record an official at-bat, finishing the day with four walks, a sacrifice hit and a sacrifice fly. Huggins winds up leading the N.L. with 116 walks.

Aug. 3—For the first time since 1901, Bresnahan pitches in a game, giving up six hits and no runs in 3⅓ innings against Brooklyn.

Oct. 15—The Cardinals end the season with a 4-1 road loss to the Cubs and finish seventh at 63-90, 40½ games behind first-place Chicago. Konetchy becomes the team's first .300 hitter in five years.

1911

Mar. 24—Cardinals owner Matthew Stanley Robison dies of a heart attack in Cleveland. His niece, **Mrs. Helene Hathaway Robison Britton**, inherits the team and becomes the first female owner of a major league franchise.

May 13—In a 19-5 victory over the Cardinals, the Giants score 13 runs in the first inning.

July 11—While his team is traveling by train to Boston, Bresnahan asks that the club's Pullman car be repositioned to the back of the train because it is too close to the noisy engine. The request is granted and shortly afterward, the train crashes down an 18-foot embankment just west of Bridgeport, Conn. The coach car that was placed where the Cardinals' Pullman had been is destroyed and 14 people are killed. Cardinal players help remove bodies and rescue the injured, then board another train to Boston, where the day's game is postponed.

Sept. 24—The Cardinals push across a run in the sixth inning of a game against Philadelphia to snap a string of 41 consecutive scoreless innings by Phillies rookie righthander Grover Cleveland Alexander.

Oct. 9—At 75-74, the Cardinals finish with a winning record for the first time since 1901. The record nets them a fifth-place finish, 22 games behind the first-place New York Giants.

1912

July 18—First baseman Konetchy has a streak of consecutive chances handled without an error end at 592 when he makes a poor throw in a game against Brooklyn.

Oct. 6—The Cardinals finish in sixth place at 63-90, 41 games behind first-place New York. One of the positives is the performance of pitcher Harry "Slim" Sallee, who goes 16-17 and is effective both as a starter and a reliever. The lanky left-hander's success comes despite the fact he is an insomniac who likes to stay up late at night to help milkmen make their rounds.

Oct. 22—With four years left on a contract that pays him $10,000 per season, Bresnahan, never a favorite of Mrs. Britton, is fired as manager and replaced by second baseman **Huggins**. Bresnahan insists the Cardinals honor his contact, and a protracted dispute ensues. Finally, in June 1913, Bresnahan is traded to the Cubs for cash.

1913

May 4—The Cardinals beat the Cubs, 10-8, in a 13-inning game at Chicago's West Side Park. Rookie manager Huggins, short of pitchers, calls on rookie outfielder Ted Cather for relief duty, then turns to Konetchy, who pitches 4⅔ innings of one-hit ball to earn the only win of his big-league career.

June 5—Former team owner Chris Von der Ahe dies in St. Louis. According to legend, Von der Ahe had the year of his death inscribed on his life-sized gravesite marker years before he died. Others contend that the story is false, yet another self-aggrandizing creation from the fertile mind of the late owner.

Oct. 5—The Cardinals win their season finale in Cincinnati, 4-1, to avoid the 100-loss mark. At 51-99, the Cardinals finish in last place, 49 games behind the first-place Giants.

1914

July 1—Righthander Casey Hageman pitches a 5-1 complete-game victory over Pittsburgh. Until the Pirates score in the ninth inning, just two runners reach second base against the 27-year-old pitcher.

Aug. 26—More than 27,000 fans cram into Robison Field, which seats 17,000, to watch a doubleheader between the Cardinals and Giants, who are in a battle for the N.L. pennant with the Braves and Cubs. The Cardinals win the opener, 1-0, but are shut out by Mathewson in the second game, 4-0.

Oct. 5—A seven-game losing streak in September ruins the Cardinals' chances of capturing their first N.L. pennant. At 81-72, St. Louis finishes in third place—its best finish since joining the N.L. A pitching staff that had allowed the most runs in the league the year before ties for the fewest allowed this year. Bill Doak leads the N.L. with a 1.72 ERA.

1915

Apr. 19—Pitcher Lee Meadows makes his major league debut, becoming the first player to wear eyeglasses regularly in the majors since 1886. Cardinals teammates call him Specs.

Aug. 30—The Cardinals lose a heartbreaker at Philadelphia, 4-3, when a ball hit by Phillies outfielder George "Possum" Whitted in the bottom of the 10th inning bounces off the wall, then off the chest of Cardinals left fielder Bob Bescher and into the stands for a bizarre game-ending home run. The Phillies' starting pitcher is Alexander, who goes on to lead the N.L. in wins, ERA, complete games, strikeouts and shutouts.

Sept. 10—Rogers Hornsby makes his big-league debut, replacing Art Butler at shortstop in the seventh inning against the Reds. Hornsby goes 0-for-2 and makes his first start four days later.

Oct. 3—The Cardinals slip to sixth place at 72-81, 18½ games behind the first-place Phillies.

1916

May 14—Hornsby hits his first major league homer, connecting off Brooklyn righthander Jeff Pfeffer in a 3-2 loss at Robison Field. It is an inside-the-park shot for Hornsby, who will hit another 300 home runs in his career.

Oct. 1—The Cardinals end the season with a 6-3 loss to the Cubs at the Chicago club's new home, Weeghman Park (later renamed Wrigley Field), and tie the Reds for last place at 60-93. St. Louis collapses down the stretch, losing 28 of its final 33 games, including the last 14 (all on the road). The Cardinals score the fewest runs in the league and allow the most. An incensed club president Schuyler Britton, husband of club owner Helene Hathaway Robison Britton, promises "a thorough housecleaning" before the start of the 1917 season.

October—Schuyler Britton's prediction eventually comes true, but he has little to do with it. Helene Britton sells the Cardinals to the team's attorney, James Jones. One of Jones' first moves changes the future of the franchise—he hires Branch Rickey away from his job as business manager of the St. Louis Browns to become the Cardinals' team president.

1917

June 11—Mike Gonzalez, usually a catcher but playing first base on this day, ends a pitching duel between Bill Doak of the Cardinals and Joe Oeschger of the Phillies by stealing home with two outs in the 15th inning to give St. Louis a 5-4 victory at Robison Field. After yielding four runs in the first inning, Doak holds the Phils scoreless over the next 14 frames.

Sept. 18—Doak pitches two complete-game victories on the same day (2-0 and 12-4).

Sept. 30—The Cardinals make a big turnaround and go 82-70 to finish third in the N.L. Hornsby hits .327 (second in the league) and leads the N.L. in triples, slugging and total bases.

Oct. 26—Huggins, disappointed with the team's new ownership, leaves the Cardinals to accept a two-year offer to manage the New York Yankees, a franchise he will lead to six pennants and three World Series titles from 1918 to 1929. The Cardinals subsequently sign minor league manager Jack Hendricks to guide the team in 1918.

1918

July 3—The old hidden-ball trick works to perfection as the last-place Cardinals defeat the first-place Cubs, 2-1, at Robison Field. With Cubs on second and third with one out in the ninth, St. Louis second baseman Bobby Fisher tricks the runner on second, Dode Paskert, into believing that he has handed the ball back to pitcher Red Ames after a conference on the mound with shortstop Hornsby. He hadn't. After returning to his position, Fisher tags the unaware Paskert as he ambles off second base. Ames then strikes out the next batter to preserve the win.

Aug. 26—Hornsby is thrown out of a game against the Giants and fined $50 by Hendricks. The two trade jabs through the press until Rickey steps in and tells them to settle their differences in private.

Sept. 2—The season is cut short because of World War I, and the team finishes in last place at 51-78.

1919

January—Rickey begins to lay the groundwork for his idea of a team-owned minor league farm system when he purchases a share of the Houston club of the Texas League. Rickey and the Cardinals will purchase other minor league teams as a way to develop and keep talent.

Jan. 26—The Cardinals announce Rickey will replace Hendricks as manager while continuing to serve as team president. One reason for the move is that the club finished last under Hendricks the year before; another, as Rickey would later claim, is to save the team a manager's salary.

Sept. 28—The Cardinals finish seventh at 54-83, 40½ games behind N.L. champion Cincinnati. Hornsby, who plays in every game, misses the batting title by three points.

Oct. 12—Rickey holds the first of his annual tryout camps for anyone interested in pursuing a career as a professional baseball player. Among those signed to contracts are first baseman **Jim Bottomley** and outfielder **Ray Blades**.

December—**Sam Breadon**, owner of the Western Automobile Co. and one of the team's larger stock holders, accepts the position of club president, with **Rickey** becoming vice president and general manager (and staying on as field manager).

BOTTOMLEY

1920

January—The Cardinals borrow $10,000 to purchase minor leaguer Jesse Haines from Kansas City. Haines had compiled a 21-5 record at Kansas City in 1919 and fashioned a 2.11 ERA. The righthander, who appeared in one game with the Cincinnati Reds in 1918, will go on to pitch 18 seasons for the Cardinals, the longest tenure of any pitcher in team history.

June 6—Breadon sells Robison Field to the St. Louis school board for $275,000 and leases the use of Sportsman's Park from Browns owner Phil Ball for $35,000 per season. He also agrees to pay half of the annual cleanup cost at the ballpark.

July 1—The Cardinals move into Sportsman's Park—their home for nearly 46 years—with a 6-2, 10-inning loss to the Pirates. This Sportsman's Park is located at the same site as Von der Ahe's first Sportsman's Park facility—on the west side of Grand between Dodier and Sullivan.

Sept. 17—The Cardinals set a major league record with 12 consecutive hits in a 9-4 victory over Boston.

Oct. 3—The Cardinals finish the season in a fifth-place deadlock with the Cubs at 75-79. Hornsby hits .370 to win the first of six consecutive batting championships. He leads the league in doubles with 44 and in runs batted in with 94. Bill Doak wins 20 games; Haines loses 20.

BLADES

1921

June 13—The Cardinals beat the Giants, 10-1, at Sportsman's Park for their club-record 10th straight victory. Center fielder Les Mann hits two home runs in support of Haines, who goes the distance for his sixth win in a row. The only negative comes in the eighth inning, when Hornsby hits into a 4-3-6 triple play.

Aug. 5—Harold Arlin is behind the microphone as the first radio broadcast of a major league game is heard over KDKA in Pittsburgh. The Pirates beat the Phillies, 8-5.

Oct. 2—The Cardinals end the season at 87-66, their highest win total since joining the N.L. They win 30 of their last 37 games to finish third, seven games behind first-place New York. Hornsby leads the league in runs, hits, doubles, RBIs and batting average. Promising young outfielder Austin McHenry hits .350, 47 points behind the Rajah but the third-best figure in the league.

1922

Feb. 23—The Cardinals are hit by stunning news: Catcher William "Pickles" Dillhoefer, a solid but unspectacular backup, is dead of pneumonia at age 27.

July 20—**Hornsby** sets a modern N.L. record with his 25th homer—a two-out, three-run shot in the bottom of the ninth to beat the Braves 7-6.

Aug. 18—Bottomley makes his major league debut.

Sept. 20—Hornsby's 33-game hitting streak, the longest in franchise history, ends against Brooklyn's Burleigh Grimes in the first game of a doubleheader at Ebbets Field.

Sept. 24—Hornsby hits his final two homers of the season—Nos. 41 and 42—in a 10-6 victory over the Giants in New York.

Oct. 1—Hornsby sets an N.L. record with 250 hits and also leads the league in homers and RBIs (152) to win the Triple Crown. The Cardinals finish in a tie for third place at 85-69.

Nov. 27—Two months after his 27th birthday, McHenry dies of a brain tumor at his Ohio home. The tumor had been discovered earlier in the season after McHenry, who had been complaining of headaches and having trouble judging fly balls in the outfield, was taken to a doctor by Rickey to get an examination.

HORNSBY

1923

July 10—Rookie Johnny Stuart pitches two complete-game victories at Braves Field in Boston (11-1 and 6-3). They are the first starts of the season and just the second and third in the career of Stuart, a former football player at Ohio State.

Aug. 12—Hornsby curses out Rickey in the visitors' clubhouse at the Polo Grounds in New York in a disagreement over strategy. According to accounts, coach Burt Shotton has to step in to keep the two apart. Rickey, his club muddling through a mediocre season, says the incident "amounted to nothing." Later in the season, Hornsby is suspended for five games after saying he is too ill to play while the team's doctors pronounce him fit.

Oct. 7—The Cardinals split a doubleheader at home against the Cubs and finish in fifth place at 79-74. Hornsby wins the batting title with a .384 average despite playing in only 107 games. Bottomley hits .371 in his first full big-league season.

1924

July 17—**Haines** no-hits Boston in a 5-0 victory at Sportsman's Park, becoming the first Cardinal to hurl a nine-inning no-hitter.

July 19—Two days after Haines' feat, Herman Bell pitches two complete-game victories on the same day (6-1 and 2-1), allowing Boston just six hits overall. The rookie, however, wins only one other game all season.

Sept. 16—In a 17-3 victory at Brooklyn, Bottomley sets a major league record with 12 RBIs in one game. (Dodgers manager Wilbert Robinson had held the record with 11, a mark he set with Baltimore in 1892.) Bottomley hit three singles, a double and two homers.

Sept. 28—The Cardinals finish the season 65-89 and tumble to sixth place. Hornsby hits .424—the highest average ever in the 20th century—but doesn't win the N.L. MVP Award when a Cincinnati writer leaves Hornsby off his ballot.

1925

Apr. 22—The Cardinals score 11 runs in the first inning of their home opener in a 12-3 win over Cincinnati. The Cards pounce on Reds starter Pete Donohue, who had shut them out a week earlier in Cincinnati.

May 30—With his team sporting a 13-25 record, Breadon fires Rickey as manager and appoints Hornsby to take his place. Rickey remains the team's vice president and farm-system director.

Sept. 27—Hornsby has five hits in a doubleheader against Boston, including his 38th and 39th homers, to raise his average to .403, the sixth consecutive year he has led the league in hitting. Hornsby sits out the final three games with a sore toe. The Cardinals go 64-51 with him as manager and finish the season 77-76, good for fourth in the league. Hornsby wins his second Triple Crown (.403, 39 HRs, 143 RBIs) and becomes the first Cardinal to win a National League Most Valuable Player Award.

1926

June 22—The Cardinals acquire **Grover Cleveland Alexander** off waivers from the Cubs.

Aug. 31—The Cardinals move into first place with a doubleheader sweep of the Pirates at Sportsman's Park.

Sept. 8—Hornsby goes into an obscenity-laced tirade against Breadon after the owner tells him he wants the team to play in a pair of exhibition games in New Haven, Conn. It's the foundation for Hornsby's eventual exit from the Cardinals.

Sept. 24—The Cardinals clinch their first N.L. pennant with a 6-4 win over the Giants in New York. A few days later, they finish the season at 89-65.

Oct. 10—The Cardinals win their first World Series with a 3-2 victory over the Yankees in Game 7 in New York. Alexander

becomes a hero when he comes out of the bullpen and strikes out Tony Lazzeri with the bases loaded and two outs in the seventh inning. The game ends with Babe Ruth being thrown out while attempting to steal second base.

Dec. 5—Catcher **Bob O'Farrell** is named N.L. MVP. Later in the month, he is named manager, succeeding Hornsby.

Dec. 20—The Cardinals trade Hornsby to the Giants for second baseman Frankie Frisch and pitcher Jimmy Ring.

1927

May 14—The Cardinals lose, 12-4, at Philadelphia's Baker Bowl, but the game is remembered for another reason. In the seventh inning, a section of the right field stands—full of fans—collapses, injuring about 50 people and causing one person to suffer a fatal heart attack.

June 18—After aviation hero Charles Lindbergh helps to raise the team's N.L. pennant in pregame ceremonies at Sportsman's Park, the Cardinals defeat the visiting Giants, 6-4.

Sept. 29—The Cardinals' hopes of repeating as World Series champions officially end with a 3-2 loss at Cincinnati. With a record of 92-61, they finish 1½ games behind Pittsburgh. Frisch strikes out just 10 times in 153 games, leads the N.L. in stolen bases (48) and finishes second in MVP voting in his first St. Louis season.

Nov. 7—Bill McKechnie, manager of the Cardinals' Rochester farm club, replaces O'Farrell as manager.

SOUTHWORTH

1928

Apr. 12—Alexander shuts down Pittsburgh, 9-0, at Sportsman's Park. It is the 90th and final shutout of his career—an N.L. record.

Sept. 20—In the first game of a doubleheader in New York, George Harper has the first three-homer game in Cardinals history.

Sept. 29—The Cardinals clinch their second N.L. pennant in three seasons with a 3-1 victory at Boston. They finish the season with a record of 95-59 and set a club record for home attendance (761,574).

Oct. 9—Babe Ruth swats three homers in a 7-3 Yankees victory in Game 4 of the World Series at Sportsman's Park as New York completes a sweep of the Cardinals.

Nov. 21—**Billy Southworth** replaces McKechnie as manager.

Dec. 2—Bottomley, who leads the N.L. in triples and RBIs and finishes tied in home runs, is voted N.L. MVP.

1929

July 6—The Cardinals end an 11-game losing streak with a 28-6 victory in the second game of a doubleheader at Philadelphia, setting a modern N.L. record for runs. The beneficiary of the onslaught, starting pitcher Fred Frankhouse, has four hits himself, as does Bottomley. Center fielder/leadoff man Taylor Douthit leads the way with five.

July 9—**Chick Hafey** ties an N.L. record with his 10th consecutive hit over two games in a 7-4 victory over the Phillies.

July 24—Oh, never mind: McKechnie, who had been replaced as manager by Southworth the previous November, replaces Southworth on the St. Louis bench.

Aug. 10—Alexander beats the team he began his career with—the Phillies—for his 373rd and final big-league win. He pitches four scoreless innings in relief before the Cardinals push across two runs in the 11th inning for an 11-9 victory. Alexander's career win total equals Mathewson's N.L. record.

Sept. 29—The Cardinals beat the Pirates, 10-2, at Sportsman's Park to finish a disappointing season at 78-74, 20 games out of first.

1930

Sept. 16—The Cardinals hand Brooklyn its first loss in 11 games—1-0 at Ebbets Field—to move into a first-place tie with the Dodgers. Pitching with a bandaged finger sticking out of his glove, Cardinals lefthander Bill Hallahan retires the first 20 batters he faces and holds the Dodgers to five hits in a complete-game victory.

Sept. 26—The Cardinals clinch the N.L. pennant with a 10-5 victory over Pittsburgh at Sportsman's Park.

Sept. 28—**Dizzy Dean** makes his major league debut on the final day of the season and throws a three-hitter to beat Pittsburgh, 3-1. Dean also singles and steals home in the third inning. While Dean has an impressive debut game,

outfielder George Watkins has an impressive debut season—his .373 batting average is the highest ever by a major league rookie. Watkins, however, does not lead the league; Giants first baseman Bill Terry hits a robust .401. All eight of St. Louis' regular position players hit .300 or better. The Cardinals finish the season with a record of 92-62 and win their third N.L. championship.

Oct. 8—The Cardinals lose the World Series in six games to the Philadelphia Athletics. An offense that produces a team-record 1,004 runs during the regular season scores just one run in the final 22 innings against the A's.

1931

Aug. 5—**Bottomley** has a day to remember against the Pirates. After collecting four hits in the first game of a doubleheader, he gets six hits in six at-bats in the nightcap. It is the second 6-for-6 performance of his career.

Sept. 16—The Cardinals clinch the N.L. pennant—their fourth in six seasons—with a 6-3 victory over the Phillies at Sportsman's Park.

Sept. 27—Hafey goes 1-for-8 on the final day of the season but wins the closest batting race in big-league history to that point. Hafey's .3489 average edges New York's Terry (.3486) and teammate Bottomley (.3482). The Cards finish with a record of 101-53, their first 100-win year.

Oct. 10—The Cardinals, now managed by Gabby Street, prevent the Athletics from winning three straight World Series, beating the A's, 4-2, in Game 7. Hallahan rescues Series standout Grimes after the A's put two runners on base with two outs in the ninth. Pepper Martin excels for St. Louis, hitting .500 with five runs, five RBIs and five stolen bases.

Oct. 20—**Frisch** (.311, 28 steals, 82 RBIs) is selected N.L. MVP.

1932

Apr. 11—Hafey, fresh off a batting title, is traded to the Reds after a contract dispute with Cardinals officials.

May 11—Hallahan lives up to his "Wild Bill" nickname by throwing a record-tying three wild pitches in one inning in a loss to Brooklyn.

Aug. 14—The Cardinals sweep a doubleheader from the Cubs at Sportsman's Park behind superb pitching by rookies Tex Carleton and Dizzy Dean.

Sept. 2—Joe Medwick makes his major league debut, going 0-for-4 for St. Louis in a game against the Cubs.

Sept. 25—The Cardinals fall to 72-82—their first losing season since 1924—and finish 18 games behind pennant-winning Chicago.

Oct. 24—Hornsby is signed by the Cardinals after being released by the Cubs. He plays in 46 games for St. Louis in 1933 and hits .325.

Dec. 17—Bottomley joins former teammate Hafey in Cincinnati via a trade. Like Hornsby, Bottomley will finish his playing career as a member of the A.L.'s St. Louis Browns in 1937.

1933

May 7—The Cardinals make a multi-player deal with the Reds and acquire light-hitting, fiery shortstop Leo Durocher.

July 2—The Cardinals fail to score a run while losing both ends of a doubleheader to the first-place Giants. Both games end 1-0 as Carl Hubbell (18) and Roy Parmelee (nine) do not allow a run in a combined 27 innings.

July 6—The Cardinals are well-represented at baseball's first All-Star Game as Frisch, Hallahan, Martin and catcher Jim Wilson all play in the game at Chicago's Comiskey Park. Frisch hits a homer for the N.L., the first of 13 that will be hit by Cardinal players in All-Star Games.

July 24—Street quits as manager and Frisch takes over. The team responds by winning 16 of its next 17 games.

July 30—Dean sets a modern major league record with 17 strikeouts in an 8-2 victory over the Cubs.

Oct. 1—The Cardinals go 82-71 and finish in fifth place. Dean, in his second full year in the majors, wins 20 games.

1934

Sept. 16—Courtesy of the **Dean brothers**, the Cardinals sweep a doubleheader from the first-place Giants before a record crowd of 62,573 at the Polo Grounds. Dizzy wins the first game, 5-3, and Paul takes the second, 3-1.

Sept. 21—Dizzy throws a three-hit shutout against the Dodgers in the first game of a doubleheader in Brooklyn but is upstaged by Paul, who throws a 3-0 no-hitter in the second game.

Sept. 30—The Cardinals clinch the N.L. pennant on the final day of the season. Dizzy shuts out the Reds, 9-0, at Sportsman's Park for his 30th victory of the season. The Cardinals finish 95-58, two games ahead of New York.

Oct. 9—The Cardinals win the World Series by clobbering the Tigers, 11-0, in Game 7 at Detroit. Fans toss garbage at left fielder Medwick, who slid high into third baseman Marv Owen in the top of the sixth, when he takes the field for the bottom of the inning. In an effort to restore order, commissioner Kenesaw Mountain Landis orders Medwick removed from the game. The Dean brothers account for all four Series wins for St. Louis.

Nov. 3—Dizzy is named N.L. MVP after leading the league in wins, strikeouts (195) and shutouts (seven).

PAUL AND DIZZY DEAN

1935

July 18—The Cardinals pound out 18 hits and Paul Dean pitches a complete game in a 13-3 romp over the Boston Braves at Sportsman's Park. It is the Cardinals' 18th straight victory at home and 14th consecutive win overall. Burgess Whitehead and Rip Collins pace the team with four hits each.

July 31—At Cincinnati, a female fan, Kitty Burke, runs on the field and grabs a bat from Reds outfielder Babe Herman as he is about to face Paul Dean. Burke hits a slow underhand toss back to the mound, and Dean throws her out at first. Frisch insists the out should count, but the umpires overrule him.

Sept. 5—Rookie Terry Moore becomes the first player in Cardinals history to go 6-for-6 in a home game. He does it against the Braves.

Sept. 27—The Cubs, battling St. Louis for the pennant, sweep a doubleheader from St. Louis at Sportsman's Park to stretch their winning streak to 21 games. The win in the opener clinches the flag for Chicago. The Cardinals end the season two days later at 96-58.

1936

Apr. 14—On opening day in St. Louis, Eddie Morgan makes baseball history, becoming the first player to hit a pinch home run in his first major league at-bat. It is the only homer Morgan hits in 39 big-league games.

Apr. 16—The Cards' **Johnny Mize** makes his big-league debut, striking out as a pinch hitter against the Cubs.

July 7—The N.L. wins its first All-Star Game, 4-3, at Braves Field in Boston as two Cardinals make major contributions. **Medwick** drives in what turns out to be the winning run in the fifth inning and Dizzy Dean, the N.L.'s starting pitcher, allows no hits in three innings to earn the victory.

July 21—Medwick ties an N.L. record when he stretches his consecutive-hit streak to 10 with singles in his first three at-bats against the Giants.

Sept. 25—Medwick hits his 64th double of the season—an N.L. record that still stands.

Sept. 27—On the season's final day, Walter Alston, who will later manage the Dodgers for 23 seasons, replaces Mize (ejected from the game) at first base and strikes out in his only major league at-bat. Cards go 87-67 and tie for second place.

1937

June 5—The Cardinals sign 16-year-old pitcher **Stan Musial** to a professional contract. He reports to the minors in 1938.

July 7—At the All-Star Game in Washington, Cleveland's Earl Averill hits a line drive that breaks Dizzy Dean's left big toe. Dean returns from the injury in September but the toe isn't fully healed. As a result, he alters his motion and injures his shoulder. Medwick sets an All-Star record with four hits.

Aug. 4—The Cardinals score five runs in the ninth to pull out a 7-6 win over Boston in St. Louis. The final two runs come home on a pinch single by Frisch, his final career hit. Medwick hits four doubles.

Oct. 3—The Cardinals, 81-73, finish fourth. Medwick wins the Triple Crown with a .374 average, 31 homers and a club-record 154 RBIs. A month later he is voted N.L. MVP.

MUSIAL

1938

Jan. 18—Grover Cleveland Alexander, a Cardinal from 1926-29, is elected to the Baseball Hall of Fame.

Apr. 16—The Cardinals trade Dizzy Dean to the Cubs for outfielder Tuck Stainback, pitchers Curt Davis and Clyde Shoun and $185,000. Dean, still just 27 years old, will win only 16 games the rest of his career.

Apr. 19—Enos Slaughter makes his big-league debut, getting three hits in St. Louis' season opener against Pittsburgh.

Aug. 2—The Cardinals lose, 6-2, to the Dodgers at Ebbets Field in the first game in which experimental yellow baseballs are used. The new balls, supposedly easier to follow, are best described by Mize (who hits one of them for a home run) as "stitched lemons."

Sept. 11—Frisch is fired as manager following a 6-4 win over the Pirates. The Cardinals, in sixth place at the time, appoint coach Mike Gonzalez to take over for the rest of the season.

Oct. 2—The Cardinals finish 71-80 and fall to sixth place, 17½ games behind first-place Chicago.

Nov. 6—Former outfielder Ray Blades, a favorite of Rickey's, is named manager of the Cardinals.

1939

Aug. 16—Moore hits two inside-the-park homers against the Pirates at Forbes Field.

Aug. 20—The Cardinals sweep a doubleheader from the Reds at Crosley Field, pull within 3½ games of the Reds in the N.L. race. Martin has three hits in each game and Mize hits two homers in the nightcap.

Sept. 28—A 5-3 loss to the Reds eliminates the Cardinals from pennant contention.

Oct. 1—The Cardinals finish in second place—4½ games behind first-place Cincinnati—with a 92-61 record. Mize wins the batting title (.349) and leads the N.L. in slugging percentage (.626) and homers (28). Slaughter, at age 23, hits .320 and leads the league with 52 doubles. Davis, one of the players acquired for Dizzy Dean the previous year, wins 22 games.

1940

May 7—The Cards hit seven homers and rout Brooklyn, 18-2.

June 4—The Cardinals lose to Brooklyn, 10-1, in their first night game in St. Louis. Medwick goes 5-for-5.

June 7—Breadon fires Blades and replaces him with minor league manager Southworth, who had been Cards manager for part of the 1929 season.

June 12—The Cardinals trade Medwick and Davis to the Dodgers for four players and $125,000. When the clubs meet six days later at Ebbets Field, Cards pitcher Bob Bowman beans Medwick, who is knocked unconscious. The incident sets off a long feud between the two clubs.

Sept. 29—The 84-69 Cards finish third. Mize leads the N.L. with 137 RBIs and a club-record 43 homers.

1941

Aug. 10—Slaughter breaks his collarbone in an outfield collision with Moore and misses the remainder of the year.

Aug. 30—**Lon Warneke** throws a 2-0 no-hitter at Cincinnati. Only three balls hit by the Reds make it to the outfield.

Sept. 17—In the second game of a doubleheader at Sportsman's Park, Musial makes his big-league debut. After popping out to third base in his first trip to the plate, he gets two hits in his next three at-bats, including a two-run double, to help the Cards beat Casey Stengel's Braves, 3-2.

Sept. 23—Musial hits the first of 475 career homers in a 9-0 victory at Pittsburgh. The blast comes against Rip Sewell.

Sept. 28—In the season finale, Johnny Beazley goes the distance in his first appearance in the majors, winning 3-1 at Chicago. The 97-56 Cards finish second, 2½ games behind Brooklyn.

Dec. 11—The Cardinals trade Mize to the Giants for three nondescript players and $50,000.

1942

HALL OF FAME

1942

Rogers Hornsby

Jan. 4—**Rogers Hornsby**, a Cardinal from 1915-26 and in 1933, is elected to the Baseball Hall of Fame.

Sept. 27—The Cards win the pennant on the final day, taking a doubleheader from the Cubs (the first game clinches it). They finish 106-48, two games ahead of Brooklyn.

Oct. 3—Lefthander Ernie White shuts out New York, 2-0, in Game 3 of the World Series at Yankee Stadium to give St. Louis a two games-to-one lead.

Oct. 5—Rookie third baseman Whitey Kurowski delivers a decisive two-run homer in the ninth inning as the Cardinals win, 4-2, to beat the heavily favored Yankees in five games. It is the Yanks' first World Series loss since the Cardinals beat them in 1926.

Oct. 29—Rickey resigns as Cardinals vice president and farm-system director. Three days later, he signs a five-year contract to head up Brooklyn's baseball operations.

Nov.—Righthanded pitcher **Mort Cooper**, who leads the league in wins, shutouts and ERA, is named N.L. MVP.

1943

Feb. 24—Because so many of their minor leaguers have enlisted in military service or been drafted, the Cardinals reduce their farm system from 21 teams to seven. The next day, the team places a classified ad in the SPORTING NEWS looking for young players.

May 31—Cooper allows just one hit—a looping double down the right field line—in a 7-0 win over Brooklyn. He throws another one-hitter in his next start, against Philadelphia on June 4.

Sept. 18—The Cardinals clinch their second consecutive N.L. pennant with a doubleheader sweep of the Cubs in St. Louis. A couple of weeks later, they end the season with a 105-49 record. Musial hits .357 to win his first batting title.

Oct. 11—The Yankees avenge their 1942 defeat by beating the Cardinals, 2-0, to close out the World Series in five games. The Cardinals score two or fewer runs in each of their four losses.

November—Musial, who leads the league in hits, doubles and triples as well as batting average, is named N.L. MVP.

1944

June 10—Cooper tosses a five-hit shutout as the Cardinals romp at Cincinnati, 18-0. The Reds become so desperate that they send a hometown kid to the mound—15-year-old lefthander Joe Nuxhall, who is the youngest player ever to appear in a major league game.

Sept. 21—The Cardinals clinch their third straight N.L. pennant with a 5-4 win over Boston. Nine days later, they finish the season with a 105-49 record, giving them 316 victories in three seasons.

Oct. 9—The Cardinals beat the Browns in an all-St. Louis World Series, clinching matters with a 3-1 victory in Game 6. The Cardinals hold their city rivals to just two runs in the final three games.

Dec. 21—Shortstop and defensive wizard **Marty Marion** is voted N.L. MVP. He also is named Major League Player of the Year by the SPORTING NEWS, the first Cardinal so honored.

MARION

1945

Jan. 22—**Musial** enlists in the U.S. Navy and misses the entire 1945 season.

Apr. 17—Red Schoendienst makes his major league debut. He plays left field in the season opener at Chicago, hits a triple in four at-bats and makes an error. He sees heavy outfield duty in '45.

May 23—The Cardinals trade Cooper, a three-time 20-game winner, to the Braves.

July 4—Outfielder Augie Bergamo collects eight hits in the Cardinals' doubleheader sweep at the Polo Grounds, 8-4 and 19-2. In the nightcap, he has two homers (one a grand slam) and eight RBIs.

Sept. 30—The Cardinals go 95-59 and finish three games behind the N.L. champion Cubs. With Musial gone, Kurowski leads the team in batting (.323), homers (21) and RBIs (102). After the season, Southworth receives a lucrative offer to manage the Boston Braves and is replaced by **Eddie Dyer**.

1946

Aug. 12—Musial goes 4-for-4 in a 5-0 victory at Chicago, giving him 12 hits in 13 at-bats over three games.

Sept. 29—The Cardinals miss a chance to win the pennant on the season's final day when they lose, 8-3, to the Cubs at Sportsman's Park and finish tied for first with Brooklyn at 96-58. A best-of-three playoff is scheduled.

Oct. 3—The Cardinals, after winning the first game, 4-2, build an early 8-1 and cruise to an 8-4 victory and two-game playoff sweep of the Dodgers.

Oct. 15—In one of the most famous plays in World Series history, **Slaughter** makes a "Mad Dash" from first base to score on Harry Walker's hit to left-center in the eighth inning, giving the Cardinals a 4-3 victory over the Red Sox in Game 7.

Nov. 22—Musial wins his second N.L. MVP award. He also is named Major League Player of the Year by the SPORTING NEWS.

1947

HALL OF FAME

1947

Frankie Frisch

Jan. 21—**Frankie Frisch**, a Cardinal from 1927-37, is elected to the Hall of Fame.

June 9—Schoendienst is 0-for-12 in a doubleheader against the Phillies.

July 30—Down 10-0 in the fourth inning, the Cardinals score six runs with two outs in the bottom of the ninth against Brooklyn to tie the game at 10-10 and send it into extra innings. The Dodgers, however, win when Pee Wee Reese singles home Gene Hermanski in the 10th.

Sept. 27—The 89-65 Cardinals finish second—five games back of Brooklyn.

Nov. 25—Breadon sells the Cardinals to two local buyers, attorney Fred Saigh and **U.S. Postmaster General Bob Hannegan.**

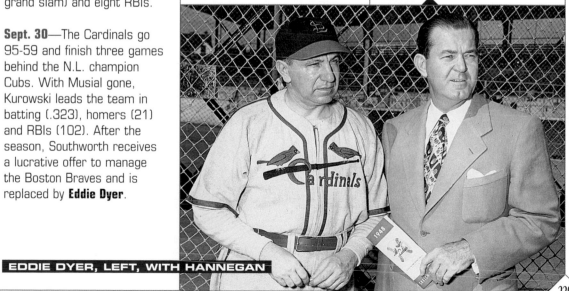

EDDIE DYER, LEFT, WITH HANNEGAN

239

1948

June 6—In a doubleheader sweep of the Phillies, **Schoendienst** ties an N.L. record with five doubles. Combined with his three doubles the previous day, he sets a major league record with eight doubles over a three-game span. Four Cardinals—Schoendienst, Slaughter, Erv Dusak and Nippy Jones—hit homers in the sixth inning of the first game.

July 13—Sportsman's Park is the All-Star Game site. Musial thrills local fans with a first-inning homer.

Aug. 29—Jackie Robinson hits for the cycle as the Dodgers beat the Cardinals, 12-7, at Sportsman's Park.

Sept. 22—Musial ties a record held by Ty Cobb with his fourth five-hit game of the season. He homers, doubles and singles three times in an 8-2 victory over the Braves.

Oct. 3—The Cardinals end the season in second place at 85-69. Musial leads the N.L. in every major hitting department except home runs.

November—Musial is the N.L. MVP for the third and last time.

1949

May 10—Breadon, owner of the Cardinals from late 1919 to late 1947, dies of cancer at age 72.

July 24—The one and only: Musial hits for the cycle for the only time in his career, accomplishing the feat in a 14-1 triumph at Brooklyn.

Sept. 29—The Cardinals fall out of first place after a 7-2 loss at Pittsburgh.

Oct. 2—The Cardinals wallop the Cubs, 13-5, at Wrigley Field on the final day of the season but lose the N.L. pennant by one game when Brooklyn beats the Phillies, 9-7, in 10 innings. St. Louis loses six of its last nine games to finish 96-58. Nevertheless, the 1940s are the winningest decade in franchise history. From 1940 through 1949, the Cardinals win 960 games and lose 580 (.623 winning percentage), cop four pennants and take three World Series championships.

1950

April 18—The Cardinals defeat the Pirates, 4-1, in the first season-opening night game in St. Louis.

May 18—Third baseman Tommy Glaviano makes four errors (three in the ninth inning) to help turn an 8-5 Cardinals lead into a 9-8 Dodgers win at Ebbets Field.

July 11—Schoendienst, an 11th-inning defensive replacement, gives the N.L. a 4-3 win in the All-Star Game with a 14th-inning homer at Comiskey Park.

July 27—Musial's 30-game hitting streak—the longest in the majors in the 1950s—ends when he is the only Cardinal to go hitless in a 13-3 thrashing of Brooklyn.

Oct. 1—The Cardinals end the season in fifth place at 78-75. Musial hits .356 and wins the batting title.

Oct. 16—Dyer resigns as manager and is replaced by longtime shortstop Marion.

1951

Sept. 13—The Cardinals become the first team in the 20th century to play two teams on the same day in the same ballpark as they play host to the Giants and Braves at Sportsman's Park. Neither game, ironically, was on the schedule at the beginning of the season. After beating the Giants, 6-4, in the opener, a makeup game from the night before, the Cardinals are beaten by the Braves, 2-0, in a makeup game from earlier in the season. Twenty-game winner Sal Maglie takes the loss in the opener for New York; 20-game winner Warren Spahn wins the nightcap for Boston.

Sept. 30—The Cardinals split a doubleheader at Chicago and finish in third place at 81-73. Musial hits .355 to win his second straight batting title. Marion is fired as manager and replaced by ▶ **Eddie Stanky.**

Nov.—Musial is named Major League Player of the Year by the SPORTING NEWS.

1952

June 15—The Cardinals rally from an 11-0 deficit to beat the Giants 14-12 in the first game of a doubleheader at the Polo Grounds. It is the largest comeback in the 76-year history of the National League. Slaughter (five RBIs) and Solly Hemus (two home runs) pace the St. Louis attack.

Sept. 28—In the season finale, Musial makes his only big-league pitching appearance. He faces one man, the Cubs' Frankie Baumholtz, who as the second batter in the first inning turns around to hit righthanded and reaches on third baseman Hemus' error. Stan is then relieved by the man he replaced, starting pitcher Harvey Haddix (who had moved to the outfield). Musial goes 1-for-3 and wins his third straight batting title, topping Baumholtz .336 to .325. The 88-66 Cards finish third.

1953

HALL OF FAME

1953

Dizzy Dean

Jan. 21—Dizzy Dean, a Cardinal in 1930 and from 1932-37, is elected to the Baseball Hall of Fame.

Jan. 28—Saigh is sentenced to 15 months in prison and fined $15,000 on charges of income tax evasion. He puts the club up for sale.

BUSCH AND COMPANY

Feb. 20—Anheuser-Busch buys the Cardinals from Saigh for $3.75 million.

April 9—Browns owner Bill Veeck sells Sportsman's Park to Anheuser-Busch Inc. for $800,000. **August A. Busch Jr.** wants to rename the stadium Budweiser Park but settles for Busch Stadium.

Sept. 25— Cardinals rookie lefthander Harvey Haddix wins his 20th game.

Sept. 27—The Cards finish in a tie for third at 83-71. Ray Jablonski hits 21 home runs, a club rookie record.

1954

Apr. 11—Slaughter is dealt to the Yankees for three players in the New York farm system—outfielders Bill Virdon and Emil Tellinger and pitcher Mel Wright.

ALSTON   MOON

Apr. 13—It's a day of firsts at Busch Stadium: First baseman **Tom Alston** becomes the first black player in Cardinals history and outfielder **Wally Moon** homers in his first big-league at-bat.

Apr. 23—It's another first: In his seventh game, Milwaukee rookie Hank Aaron hits his first career homer—a seventh-inning shot off Cards righthander Vic Raschi.

May 2—Musial hits five home runs in a doubleheader against the Giants in St. Louis, connecting three times in the first game and twice in the second. Alston is 4-for-4 in the opener but few notice.

Sept. 26—The Cardinals finish 72-82 and drop to sixth place. Moon is named N.L. Rookie of the Year.

1955

May 27—Stanky wreaks havoc on the visiting clubhouse at Crosley Field after a loss to the Reds and is fired the next day by Busch. Rochester manager Harry Walker is hired as Stanky's replacement.

June 1—It's rookie day at Pittsburgh's Forbes Field as Ken Boyer and Bill Virdon get three hits apiece and lefthander Luis Arroyo pitches a six-hit, 6-2 victory over the Pirates. It is Arroyo's sixth win without a loss. Pittsburgh rookie outfielder Roberto Clemente goes 1-for-3 and drives in a run.

July 12—Musial ends the All-Star Game in dramatic fashion, homering in the bottom of the 12th at Milwaukee's County Stadium for a 6-5 N.L. triumph.

Sept. 25—The Cardinals finish in seventh at 68-86—their lowest win total since 1924.

Oct. 6—The Cardinals hire Frank Lane as general manager. Six days later, Lane fires Walker and replaces him with Fred Hutchinson.

1956

G.M. Lane takes the birds-on-the-bat logo off the front of the Cardinals' uniforms. Fans are incensed. The familiar logo returns in 1957. At right is **Don Blasingame**, who in the 1956 season replaces Schoendienst as the Cards' second baseman.

June 14—One month after trading Virdon, the reigning N.L. Rookie of the Year, to Pittsburgh in a questionable deal, Lane lives up to his "Trader Lane" nickname by shipping four players, including the highly popular Schoendienst, to the Giants for four players. Shortstop Alvin Dark and outfielder Whitey Lockman are among those joining St. Louis.

July 9—The SPORTING NEWS selects Musial as its Player of the Decade for 1946-55.

Sept. 30—One day after knocking the Milwaukee Braves out of first place, the Cards finish the season in fourth place at 76-78, 17 games behind Brooklyn.

Nov. 27—Outfielder **Charlie Peete**, the 1956 American Association batting champion, dies in a plane crash in Venezuela. The Cardinals prospect, who batted .192 in 23 games for St. Louis in '56, is killed 34 years to the day after Austin McHenry's death. Both players were 27 years old.

1957

June 21—In his first career start, **Von McDaniel**, an 18-year-old righthander right out of the Oklahoma high school ranks, holds the Dodgers to two hits in a 2-0 win at Busch Stadium.

July 28—McDaniel narrowly misses a perfect game in the first game of a doubleheader against the Pirates at Busch Stadium. The only batter to reach base is Pittsburgh's Gene Baker, who hits a bloop double down the left field line in the second inning that left fielder Del Ennis can't track down. The Cards win, 4-0.

Sept. 23—The Braves beat the Cardinals, 4-2, on a two-run homer by Aaron in the 11th inning to win the N.L. pennant. The Cardinals end the season a week later in second place at 87-67. Musial hits .351 to win his seventh and final batting title.

Nov. 12—After two tumultuous seasons as general manager, Lane resigns and is replaced by **Bing Devine**, a former public relations man for the team.

1958

Jan. 29—Musial signs a $100,000 contract, becomes top-paid player in N.L. history.

May 13—At Wrigley Field, Musial, in a pinch-hitting role, doubles off Moe Drabowsky for career hit No. 3,000. Hutchinson had given Musial the day off in the hope he could get the milestone hit during a homestand that was to begin the next night.

Sept. 1—Lefthander **Vinegar Bend Mizell** walks nine batters in a 1-0 victory over the Reds. It's the most bases on balls ever issued by an N.L. pitcher in a shutout win.

Sept. 29—The Cardinals conclude the season in a tie for fifth place at 72-82. Hutchinson is dismissed.

1959

Apr. 16—New manager Solly Hemus uses a record 25 players in a 7-6 loss to the Dodgers in Los Angeles. One of them is 23-year-old righthander Bob Gibson, who allows three hits in just one-third of an inning. A day earlier, Gibson gave up two homers in relief in his major league debut.

June 21—Musial hits the 652nd double of his career in a game against the Pirates to break Honus Wagner's N.L. record.

July 30—Gibson gets his first major league victory—a 1-0 shutout at Cincinnati.

Sept. 27—The Cardinals sweep a doubleheader from the Giants at Busch Stadium to end the season in seventh place at 71-83. One of the few highlights is outfielder **Joe Cunningham**, who makes the N.L. All-Star team and hits .345 to finish second in the batting race.

1960

Jan. 21—Musial asks for and receives a $20,000 pay cut after what he feels was a subpar 1959 season.

Apr. 12—The Cardinals lose, 3-1, to the Giants in the inaugural game at San Francisco's Candlestick Park.

May 15—In the second game of a doubleheader at Wrigley Field, Chicago's Don Cardwell throws a 4-0 no-hitter against the Cardinals.

May 28—The Cardinals trade Mizell to the Pirates in a four-player deal that brings second baseman Julian Javier to St. Louis.

Oct. 2—The Cardinals jump to third place with an 86-68 record but finish nine games back of pennant-winning Pittsburgh.

1961

July 6—Hemus is fired as manager and replaced by coach **Johnny Keane**, a 17-year member of the St. Louis organization. The first thing Keane does is put Gibson in the starting rotation.

July 17-18—**Bill White** goes 14-for-18 in back-to-back doubleheaders against the Cubs. The first day, he goes 8-for-10; the second, he is 6-for-8. White's 14 hits over two days tie a major league record held by Ty Cobb, who, ironically, dies on the first day of White's hitting onslaught. The Cardinals win all four games.

Aug. 3—The Cardinals suffer their worst shutout defeat ever—a 19-0 shellacking at Pittsburgh.

Oct. 1—At 80-74, the Cardinals finish the season in fifth place, 13 games behind league champion Cincinnati.

1962

Apr. 11—The Cardinals beat New York, 11-4, at Busch Stadium in the Mets' debut game in the National League and hand future Cardinal Roger Craig the first of his league-high 24 defeats.

May 19—Musial gets career hit No. 3,431 to surpass Honus Wagner for the top spot on the N.L.'s all-time hit list.

July 25—Musial drives in the 1,861st run of his career, breaking Mel Ott's N.L. record for RBIs.

Sept. 23—Maury Wills of the Dodgers ties and then breaks Cobb's long-standing record for most stolen bases in a season, getting his 96th and 97th in St. Louis.

Sept. 30—The Cardinals beat the Dodgers, 1-0, on a Gene Oliver home run to sweep a three-game series in Los Angeles. Oliver's shot forces a one-game playoff between the Dodgers and the Giants for the N.L. pennant. St. Louis finishes sixth in the new 10-team league at 84-78.

Nov. 19—The Cards acquire shortstop Dick Groat, the 1960 N.L. MVP, from the Pirates.

Musial, known for his unusual but highly effective batting stance, celebrated with teammates (below) after he broke the N.L. record for career hits in a game at Los Angeles.

1963

Aug. 12—It's the end of an era: Musial announces his retirement, effective at the end of the season.

Sept. 18—The league-leading Dodgers beat the second-place Cardinals, 6-5, in 13 innings at Busch Stadium to complete a three-game sweep. St. Louis falls four games behind.

Sept. 25—The Cardinals announce Musial's No. 6 will be retired and that he will become a team vice president after the season.

Sept. 29—On Stan Musial Day at Busch Stadium, Musial ends his career with two hits, bringing his total to 3,630, second only to Cobb. One of the hits is a single that eludes Reds rookie second baseman Pete Rose, who will accumulate a few hits of his own. The 93-69 Cards finish in second place.

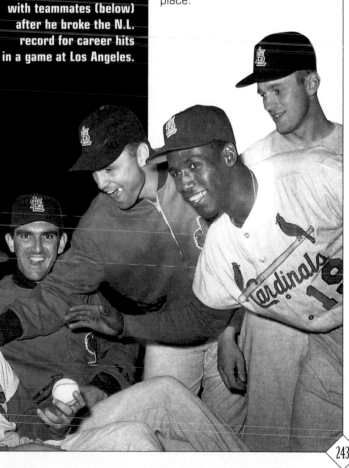

1964

June 15—With his team in eighth place and apparently going nowhere, Devine makes his boldest trade, sending pitchers **Ernie Broglio** and Bobby Shantz and outfielder Doug Clemens to the Cubs for outfielder Lou Brock and two pitchers.

Aug. 16—**Curt Flood** gets hits in eight consecutive at-bats in a doubleheader vs. Los Angeles.

Aug. 17—Busch fires Devine and appoints Bob Howsam general manager.

Oct. 4—On the final day of the season, the Cardinals beat the Mets, 11-5, to win their first N.L. pennant since 1946. Their 93-69 record places them one game ahead of the Phillies and the Reds. Boyer, the eventual N.L. MVP, leads the league with 119 RBIs. Brock hits .348 with 33 stolen bases after joining St. Louis.

Oct. 11—With the Cardinals down 2-1 in the World Series and trailing 3-0 in the sixth inning of Game 4 at Yankee Stadium, Boyer hits a grand slam to give St. Louis a 4-3 win over the Yankees.

Oct. 12—Tim McCarver hits a three-run homer in the 10th inning to give the Cardinals a 5-2 win in Game 5.

Oct. 15—The Cardinals win their first World Series in 18 years with a 7-5 victory in Game 7 at Busch Stadium.

Oct. 16—In a bizarre series of events that begins this day, Keane, still upset with the firing of Devine and hearing rumors that Busch has been courting Leo Durocher to replace him in the Cardinals dugout, announces his resignation as manager. Keane then becomes manager of the team he just defeated—the Yankees—following the dismissal of Yogi Berra in New York. Schoendienst is later named Keane's successor in St. Louis.

Cardinals fans rejoice after the team wins its first N.L. pennant since 1946.

1965

June 8—The Cardinals make righthanded pitcher Joe DiFabio their first-ever amateur draft pick. DiFabio never pitches in the majors.

Sept. 29—Gibson hits his fifth homer of the season—a grand slam off San Francisco's Gaylord Perry—in an 8-6 Cardinals win.

Oct. 3—The Cardinals win their season finale at Houston but finish in seventh place with a record of 80-81.

Oct. 20—The Cardinals trade Boyer, a World Series hero 12 months earlier, to the Mets for lefthander Al Jackson and infielder Charley Smith.

Oct. 27—The Cardinals trade White, Groat and catcher Bob Uecker to the Phillies for outfielder Alex Johnson, catcher Pat Corrales and righthander Art Mahaffey.

Dec. 8—Branch Rickey dies in Columbia, Mo., at age 83.

1966

May 8—The Cardinals play their final game at old Busch Stadium (formerly Sportsman's Park) and lose to the Giants, 10-5. They trade pitcher Ray Sadecki to the Giants for first baseman Orlando Cepeda.

May 12—The Cardinals open new Busch Memorial Stadium with a come-from-behind 4-3 victory over Atlanta in 12 innings. The crowd of 46,048 is a bit below capacity on a chilly night but nonetheless is the largest ever to see a sporting event in St. Louis.

Home plate is moved from old Busch Stadium to the new one.

July 12—The National League beats the A.L., 2-1, in 10 innings, in the first All-Star Game held in St. Louis in nine years. It's a steamy-hot day.

Sept. 28—Larry Jaster shuts out the Dodgers for the fifth time in five starts. In 45 innings against the St. Louis lefthander, the Dodgers get 24 hits, all singles. Jaster goes 6-5 with a 4.64 ERA against the rest of the league.

Oct. 3—The Cardinals finish the season in sixth place at 83-79.

Dec. 8—The Cardinals trade Smith to the Yankees for outfielder **Roger Maris**.

MARIS

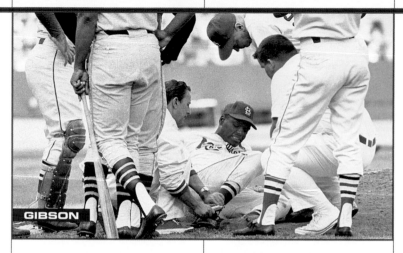

GIBSON

1967

Jan. 23—Howsam resigns as general manager and is replaced by Musial.

July 15—A vicious line drive off the bat of Pittsburgh's Roberto Clemente breaks **Gibson's** right leg in a 6-4 loss to Pittsburgh at Busch Stadium.

Sept. 18—Gibson, in his third start since the injury, clinches the pennant for the Cards with a 5-1 win at Philadelphia.

Oct. 1—The Cardinals beat Atlanta, 5-2, to finish with their first 100-win season (101-60) in 23 years. Cepeda will later be voted the first unanimous N.L. MVP.

Oct. 12—The Cardinals beat the Red Sox, 7-2, in Game 7 of the World Series at Fenway Park as Gibson homers and strikes out 10. It is his third complete game of the Series.

Dec. 5—**Musial** (below, left) resigns as general manager and is replaced by **Devine**. Musial remains with the team as a senior vice president and consultant.

1968

Jan. 23—**Joe Medwick**, a Cardinal from 1932-40 and 1947-48, is elected to the Baseball Hall of Fame.

Joe Medwick

Aug. 19—Gibson wins his 15th game in a row. The streak includes five straight shutouts.

Sept. 18—Ray Washburn throws a no-hitter against the Giants in San Francisco, one day after the Giants' Gaylord Perry no-hits the Cards.

Sept. 27—In his final start of the season, Gibson hurls his 13th shutout and lowers his ERA to a record 1.12. Two days later, the Cards finish at 97-65. They repeat as N.L. champs.

Oct. 2—In Game 1 of the World Series, Gibson strikes out 17 Tigers, a Series record.

Oct. 10—The Tigers rally from a three-games-to-one deficit to win the World Series.

Oct. 28—Gibson is unanimously voted the N.L. Cy Young Award and later is named N.L. MVP.

1969

Stan Musial

Jan. 21—**Stan Musial**, a Cardinal from 1941-63 (he missed the '45 season because of military duty), is elected to the Baseball Hall of Fame.

Mar. 17—The Cardinals trade former MVP Cepeda to the Braves for catcher/first baseman **Joe Torre**, a future MVP.

Apr. 14—Light-hitting Cardinals shortstop Dal Maxvill hits the first home run in the first major league game ever played in Canada. But the Cards still lose, 8-7, to the Expos at Montreal's Jarry Park.

Sept. 15—Steve Carlton sets a major league record with 19 strikeouts in a game against the Mets at Busch Stadium but loses, 4-3, as Ron Swoboda hits a pair of two-run homers.

Oct. 2—In baseball's first season of divisional play, the Cardinals finish fourth at 87-65 in the six-team N.L. East.

Oct. 7—The Cardinals trade Flood, McCarver, pitcher Joe Hoerner and outfielder Byron Browne to the Phillies for first baseman Dick Allen, pitcher Jerry Johnson and infielder Cookie Rojas. Flood, after 12 seasons with the Cardinals, refuses to be a part of the deal and decides to take the matter to court.

1970

Jesse Haines

Feb 1.—**Jesse Haines**, a Cardinal from 1920-37, is elected to the Hall of Fame by the Veterans Committee.

Jan. 16—Flood files a suit challenging major league baseball's reserve clause.

Mar. 10—Synthetic turf is installed at Busch Stadium.

Apr. 26—Gibson strikes out 15 batters, including six in succession, in a 4-1 victory over the Reds.

May 21—Carlton strikes out 16 but gets no decision in a 4-3 St. Louis loss at Philadelphia. Two days later, Gibson strikes out 16 Phillies and the Cardinals win, 3-1, on a pair of homers by Allen.

Oct. 1—The Cards lose to Pittsburgh, finish fourth (76-86). A month later, Gibson (23-7, 3.12 ERA) wins his second Cy Young Award.

1971

HALL OF FAME

Chick Hafey
1971

Jan. 31—**Chick Hafey**, a Cardinal from 1924-31, is elected to the Baseball Hall of Fame by the Veterans Committee.

June 8—The Cardinals take first baseman **Keith Hernandez** in the 42nd round of the amateur draft.

Aug. 4—Gibson earns career victory No. 200 in a 7-2 win over the Giants in St. Louis.

Aug. 14—Gibson, who will finish his career with two one-hitters, eight two-hitters and 24 three-hitters, pitches his only no-hitter, an 11-0 rout of the Pirates. The Cardinals score five runs in the top of the first inning to give their ace an early lead. Gibson strikes out one of the most feared batsmen in the game, Willie Stargell, for the final out.

Sept. 30—The Cardinals finish second in the N.L. East with a record of 90-72. Torre hits .363 to win the batting title and leads the league with 137 RBIs. He is voted N.L. MVP on November 10 and is later named Major League Player of the Year by the SPORTING NEWS.

1972

Feb. 25—The Cardinals make perhaps their worst trade as they send Carlton—embroiled in a contract dispute with owner Gussie Busch—to the Phillies for righthander **Rick Wise**. Wise is gone from St. Louis within two years while Carlton wins four Cy Young Awards with Philadelphia.

Apr. 15—Another bad trade: The Cardinals deal lefthanded pitcher Jerry Reuss, a St. Louis native, to the Astros for righthander Scipio Spinks and lefthander Lance Clemons. Reuss will total 220 victories over 22 big-league seasons; Spinks and Clemons will combine for nine career wins.

Aug. 29—Giants pitcher Jim Barr retires the first 20 batters he faces in a 3-0 win over the Cardinals, stretching his string of consecutive batters retired to 41, a major league record.

Oct. 4—The Cardinals beat the Pirates, 4-3, in Pittsburgh to finish in fourth place at 75-81. Gibson, in addition to winning 19 games, hits five home runs, just 11 fewer than team leader Ted Simmons.

1973

June 13—Wise is two outs away from a no-hitter before giving up a single to the Reds' Joe Morgan. The Cardinals win, 8-0, as Simmons goes 4-for-5 and Luis Melendez hits a grand slam.

Sept. 29—Gibson and the Cardinals beat Carlton and the Phillies, 7-1. The Cardinals end the season the following day at 81-81. Still, they finish only 1½ games behind the first-place Mets.

Oct. 26—Devine trades Wise and outfielder Bernie Carbo to the Red Sox for outfielder Reggie Smith and pitcher Ken Tatum.

1974

HALL OF FAME

Jim Bottomley
1974

Jan. 28—**Jim Bottomley**, a Cardinal from 1922-32, is elected to the Baseball Hall of Fame by the Veterans Committee.

July 17—Gibson strikes out Cincinnati's Cesar Geronimo for his 3,000th career strikeout, becoming the only pitcher other than Walter Johnson at that point in history to reach the 3,000 mark. On the same day, former Cardinals great Dizzy Dean dies at age 63 in Reno, Nev.

Sept. 10—It's a bad day for Maury Wills and Max Carey at Busch Stadium as Brock steals his 104th and 105th bases of the season to first tie and then break Wills' single-season record. The two steals give Lou 740 in his career, breaking Carey's longstanding N.L. record of 738.

Sept. 11—The Cardinals and Mets play on and on at Shea Stadium before rookie **Bake McBride** scores the winning run from first base on two Mets errors to give St. Louis a 4-3 win in 25 innings.

Oct. 2—The 86-75 Cardinals, trailing the Pirates by one game, are snowed out in their season finale with Montreal. A makeup game isn't necessary as the Pirates beat the Cubs in extra innings to win the N.L. East.

Nov. 27—McBride is voted N.L. Rookie of the Year. Brock, on the heels of his record-breaking 118-steal season, is later named Major League Player of the Year by the SPORTING NEWS.

1975

Sept. 1—Gibson, who has announced this will be his last season, is honored on Bob Gibson Day in front of a sellout crowd at Busch Stadium. He makes his final pitching appearance in relief two days later and ends his career with 251 victories, 3,117 strikeouts and a record 303 consecutive starts.

Sept. 28—The Cardinals end an 82-80 season with a 6-2 victory over division champion Pittsburgh to finish in a tie for third place.

1976

Apr. 19—McBride goes 5-for-8 in the Cardinals' 4-3, 17-inning loss to the Mets.

May 22—Smith hits three homers and drives in five runs in leading the Cardinals to a 7-6 win at Philadelphia.

Oct. 3—The Cardinals close out a miserable season by being shut out, 1-0, in both ends of a doubleheader against Pittsburgh. The Cardinals, who also were shut out, 8-0, the day before, end the season with a four-game losing streak and finish with a record of 72-90. It is St. Louis' first 90-loss season since 1916. Schoendienst subsequently is fired after 12 seasons as manager and replaced by minor league manager **Vern Rapp**.

1977

May 9—Lefthanded reliever Al Hrabosky walks the tightrope twice and survives both times as he defeats the defending World Series champion Reds, 6-5, in a 10-inning game at Busch Stadium. After the Reds load the bases with none out in the ninth inning, the "Mad Hungarian" strikes out George Foster, Johnny Bench and Bob Bailey in succession. Hrabosky escapes another jam in the 10th, then Ted Simmons ends the game with a homer in the bottom of the inning.

Aug. 29—Brock breaks Ty Cobb's modern major league stolen-base record by swiping No. 893 in a 4-3 loss at San Diego.

Sept. 30—Brock gets steal No. 900 in a 7-2 victory over the Mets in the first game of a doubleheader at Busch Stadium.

Oct. 2—At 83-79, the Cards finish third, 18 games behind division titlist Philadelphia. Shortstop Garry Templeton ends his first full season with 18 triples, the most in the majors since 1957.

Dec. 8—The Cardinals trade Hrabosky to Kansas City for righthander Mark Littell and catcher Buck Martinez.

1978

Apr. 16—Bob Forsch throws the first no-hit game in Busch Stadium history as he beats the Phillies, 5-0. It is the first no-hitter thrown in St. Louis in 54 years.

Apr. 25—Rapp is fired and Jack Krol acts as interim manager until Boyer, who is managing at Class AAA Rochester in the Orioles' farm system, is hired April 29.

May 26—The Cards acquire outfielder **George Hendrick** from the Padres for righthander Eric Rasmussen.

May 30—Silvio Martinez, acquired from the White Sox the previous offseason, pitches an 8-2 one-hitter against the Mets in his first start in a Cardinals uniform. The rookie also one-hits Pittsburgh July 8 and throws a pair of two-hitters but finishes just 9-8.

June 16—Tom Seaver throws the only no-hitter of his career, against St. Louis in Cincinnati.

Oct. 1—The Cardinals go 62-82 under Boyer and finish the season in fifth place at 69-93.

1979

May 1—With the Cardinals trailing Houston, 6-3, in the bottom of the 11th at Busch, pinch hitter Roger Freed hits an electrifying, game-winning grand slam with two out.

Aug. 13—Brock joins the 3,000-hit club when he lashes a line drive off the hand of Cubs righthander Dennis Lamp in a 3-2 victory at Busch Stadium. Almost overlooked is the major league debut of Tommy Herr.

Sept. 23—Brock steals the 938th and final base of his career in a 7-4 victory against the Mets at Shea Stadium and moves past turn-of-the-century player Billy Hamilton for No. 1 on the all-time list.

Sept. 28—Templeton gets three hits batting righthanded in a 7-6 loss to the Mets to give the switch hitter 100 hits from each side of the plate, a major league first.

Sept. 30—The Cardinals improve to 86-76, finish third.

Nov. 13—Hernandez, the N.L.'s leading hitter (.344), is named co-MVP with Pittsburgh's Willie Stargell, the first time the award is split.

1980

June 8—Boyer is fired by G.M. John Claiborne between games of a doubleheader in Montreal, with Krol taking over as interim manager. The next day, **Whitey Herzog**, who had won three division titles in Kansas City, is hired as the new St. Louis manager.

Aug. 29—Herzog replaces the since-fired Claiborne as general manager, with Schoendienst becoming interim manager.

Oct. 5—The Cardinals finish a forgettable season in fourth place, at 74-88.

Dec. 8—Herzog, now in the role of general manager and field manager (a job he reassumes after the season), completes an 11-player deal with the Padres, with closer Rollie Fingers being St. Louis' biggest catch. Fingers, however, is a Cardinal for only four days before Herzog sends him, Simmons and pitcher Pete Vuckovich to the Brewers for outfielder Sixto Lezcano, pitchers Lary Sorensen and Dave LaPoint and minor league outfielder David Green. The acquisition of All-Star closer Bruce Sutter from the Cubs on December 9 makes Fingers expendable; Simmons soon will be replaced by free-agent signee Darrell Porter, a Herzog favorite with the Royals.

1981

Bob Gibson

Johnny Mize

Jan. 15—**Bob Gibson**, a Cardinal from 1959-75, is elected to the Hall of Fame. Two months later, the Veterans Committee adds **Johnny Mize**, a Cardinal from 1936-41.

June 7—The Cards trade outfielder Tony Scott to Houston for pitcher Joaquin Andujar.

June 12—Major league players goes on strike. The sport is shut down for nearly two months.

Aug. 26—Templeton makes obscene gestures toward the stands before and after being ejected from a game against the Giants. Herzog fines Templeton and suspends him indefinitely. Templeton makes a public apology, but his days with the team are numbered.

Oct. 4—The regular season, split in half because of the strike, ends. The Cards' 59-43 overall mark tops the N.L. East, but they fail to finish first in either half and thereby don't qualify for the playoffs.

Nov. 20—In a three-way deal involving the Phillies and Indians, the Cardinals acquire outfielder Lonnie Smith.

After shutting down the powerful Brewers in the final two innings of Game 7 of the 1982 World Series, closer Bruce Sutter took center stage. Sutter and the Cardinals had just captured St. Louis' ninth World Series championship.

1982

Feb. 11—The Cardinals trade Templeton to San Diego for shortstop Ozzie Smith.

Aug. 22—Third-string catcher Glenn Brummer—arguably the slowest player on the team—steals home with two out in the bottom of the 12th inning, giving the Cardinals a stunning 5-4 victory over the Giants.

Sept. 19—After sweeping a pair of doubleheaders the previous two days, the Cardinals beat the Mets for the fifth time in three days, 3-1, in New York. The latest win increases their lead over second-place Philadelphia to 4½ games.

Sept. 27—The Cardinals clinch their first N.L. East title with a 4-2 victory in Montreal. The game is highlighted by a three-run, inside-the-park homer by rookie outfielder Willie McGee. Six days later,

the Cardinals end the season with a 92-70 record.

Oct. 10—The Cardinals win, 6-2, in Atlanta to complete a three-game sweep of the Braves in the National League Championship Series.

Oct. 15—In Game 3 of the World Series at Milwaukee's County Stadium, McGee hits

two homers and takes two homers away from the Brewers with leaping catches at the wall in a 6-2 St. Louis victory.

Oct. 20—The Cardinals, down 3-1 in Game 7, rally for three runs in the sixth inning and go on to a 6-3 victory over Milwaukee for the franchise's ninth World Series championship.

1983

Apr. 6—Herzog steps down as general manager and Joe McDonald takes over. But the final decisions on all personnel matters still rest with Herzog.

June 15—In an unpopular trade, Herzog sends Hernandez to the Mets for pitchers Neil Allen and Rick Ownbey.

Sept. 23—Carlton, in yet another reminder for St. Louis fans of what might have been, beats the Cardinals, 6-2, at Busch Stadium for his 300th career win.

Sept. 26—Forsch becomes the only pitcher in Cardinals history to throw two no-hitters as he tames the Expos in a 3-0 win in St. Louis.

Oct. 2—The Cardinals fall to 79-83 and fourth place, but **Lonnie Smith** hits .321 to finish second in the N.L. batting race.

1984

May 12—Cincinnati righthander Mario Soto holds the Cardinals hitless until the ninth inning, when Hendrick—mired in a deep slump—spoils Soto's fun by swatting a two-out, two-strike homer. The Reds win the game in the bottom of the ninth, 2-1.

June 23—In a nationally televised game at Wrigley Field, McGee and Cubs second baseman Ryne Sandberg put on an amazing hitting display in a game eventually won by Chicago, 12-11, in 11 innings. While McGee hits for the cycle and drives in six runs, Sandberg has five hits, seven RBIs and twice saves the Cubs from defeat by hitting game-tying homers off Sutter in the ninth and 10th innings.

Sept. 28—Sutter ties Dan Quisenberry's one-year-old major league record as he records his 45th save of the season in a 4-1 win over the Cubs.

Sept. 30—The Cardinals finish in third place at 84-78.

Dec. 7—Sutter signs a lucrative free-agent contract with Atlanta.

Dec. 12—The Cardinals trade Hendrick and minor league catcher Steve Barnard to the Pirates for lefthander **John Tudor** ◀ and catcher Brian Harper.

HALL OF FAME
1985
Lou Brock

HALL OF FAME
1985
Enos Slaughter

1985

Jan. 7—**Lou Brock**, a Cardinal from 1964-79, is elected to the Hall of Fame. Two months later, **Enos Slaughter**, a Cardinal from 1938-42 and 1946-53, is elected by the Veterans Committee.

Feb. 1—The Cardinals acquire first baseman Jack Clark from the Giants for four players.

Aug. 1—The Cards steal four bases on one pitch at Chicago as rookie Vince Coleman steals third and home and McGee second and third.

Sept. 11—Newly acquired Cesar Cedeno, subbing for the injured Clark, hits a 10th-inning homer off Mets pitcher Jesse Orosco to give the Cardinals a crucial 1-0 win at Shea Stadium. The blast makes a winner of Tudor, who goes the distance for his third straight shutout, and moves St. Louis back into a tie with the Mets for first place. Cedeno winds up hitting .434 for the Cards in 28 games.

Oct. 5—The Cards beat the Cubs, clinching the N.L. East flag with one day left in the season as Tudor earns his 20th victory in 21 decisions. The Cardinals win 100 games (101-61) for the first time in 18 years, and their 314 steals are the most by any team since 1912. McGee hits .353 to win the batting title. Tudor and Andujar both win 21 games; **Danny Cox** ◀ goes 18-9.

Oct. 14—Ozzie Smith shocks everyone by hitting his first lefthanded homer as a major leaguer, connecting off Dodgers reliever Tom Niedenfuer in the bottom of the ninth inning of Game 5 of the NLCS. The blast gives the Cardinals a 3-2 victory and a 3-2 series lead. The day before, Cardinals rookie speedster Vince Coleman was injured prior to Game 4 when the automatic tarpaulin at Busch Stadium rolled up his leg. Coleman missed the rest of the postseason.

Oct. 16—With a base open and a 5-4 lead in the ninth, Dodgers manager Tommy Lasorda elects to pitch to Clark, who rips a Niedenfuer offering for a three-run homer, giving St. Louis a 7-5 win and a trip to the World Series.

Oct. 26—The Cardinals suffer perhaps their most heartbreaking World Series defeat—a 2-1 loss to the cross-state Royals in Game 6. Kansas City rallies for two runs in the ninth inning, with a blown call at first base by umpire Don Denkinger, a misjudged pop foul by Clark, a passed ball by Porter and a two-run single by Dane Iorg doing in the Cards. St. Louis then gets blasted in Game 7 the next night, 11-0.

Nov. 18—McGee is voted N.L. MVP. Nine days later, Coleman—who steals a rookie-record 110 bases—becomes the fourth unanimous N.L. Rookie of the Year.

1986

Apr. 12—Tudor beats the Expos, 6-3, for his 18th consecutive victory at Busch Stadium.

Aug. 10—Righthander Todd Worrell records his 24th save of the season in a 5-4 triumph over the Pirates to set a major league rookie record.

Sept. 15—Mike Laga, batting against the Mets' Ron Darling, achieves a first by hitting a ball out of Busch Stadium. One problem: It was a foul ball down the right field line. Laga struck out on the next pitch.

Oct. 5—The Cardinals fall to 79-82 and finish in third place—28½ games behind the division champion Mets.

Nov. 24—**Worrell** is named N.L. Rookie of the Year.

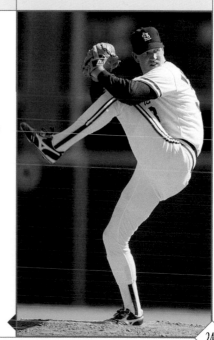

1987

Apr. 1—The Cardinals acquire catcher Tony Pena from the Pirates for three players, including outfielder Andy Van Slyke.

Apr. 18—Herr makes his first homer of the season a memorable one: a game-winning grand slam off Orosco to beat the Mets, 12-8 in 10 innings, at Busch Stadium. Fans celebrate by heaving the freebies they receive on Seat Cushion Night into the air and onto the field.

Sept. 11—The Cardinals score two runs in the ninth inning and two more in the 10th for an improbable 6-4 win over the Mets at Shea Stadium. Third baseman Terry Pendleton delivers the biggest blow—a two-run, two-out homer off reliever Roger McDowell in the ninth inning that sends the game into extra innings. The victory gives the struggling Cardinals a 2½-game lead over second-place New York.

Oct. 1—The Cardinals wrap up their third division title in six seasons with an 8-2 victory over the Expos. Three days later, St. Louis, which draws more than three million fans for the first time, ends the season with a 95-67 record.

Oct. 13—Down three games to two in the NLCS, the Cardinals rally to beat the Giants, 1-0, behind Tudor in Game 6. The next night, they win the series as righthander Danny Cox pitches a complete-game victory in Game 7.

Oct. 21—The Cardinals lose a seven-game World Series to Minnesota. The most memorable moment: Game 4, when backup infielder **Tom Lawless** (.080 hitter during the regular season) drives a Frank Viola pitch over the left field wall at Busch Stadium for only his second homer as a major leaguer. It gives the Cards a 4-1 lead. Lawless then flips his bat into the air, slugger-style, before beginning his home run trot. Lawless' antics send the packed Busch Stadium crowd into a frenzy.

1988

Jan. 6—Clark signs as a free agent with the Yankees.

Jan. 14—The Cardinals sign free agent Bob Horner, a former N.L. Rookie of the Year, as a replacement for Clark.

Apr. 22—The Cardinals trade Herr to the Twins for outfielder Tom Brunansky.

May 14—Infielder Jose Oquendo becomes the first position player to earn a pitching decision in 20 years in a 7-5, 19-inning loss to the Braves.

Aug. 16—The Cardinals trade Tudor to the Dodgers for outfielder **Pedro Guerrero.**

Sept. 24—Oquendo plays catcher in the seventh inning of a game against the Mets to become the first N.L. player since 1918 to play all nine positions in one season.

Oct. 2—At 76-86, the fifth-place Cardinals finish 25 games behind the division champion Mets. Joe Magrane (2.18) becomes the first Cardinal since John Denny in 1976 to lead the league in ERA.

1989

HALL OF FAME

1989

Red Schoendienst

Feb. 28—**Red Schoendienst**, a Cardinal from 1945-56 and 1961-63 and the team's manager from 1965-76, is elected to the Baseball Hall of Fame by the Veterans Committee.

July 28—Coleman has his major league record for consecutive stolen bases end at 50 when he is thrown out by Montreal's Nelson Santovenia in a game at Busch Stadium.

Sept. 8—A three-run homer by Pedro Guerrero is the big blow as the Cardinals rally from a 7-1 deficit to beat the Cubs, 11-8, at Wrigley Field to move to within a half-game of first-place Chicago in the N.L. East. The Cardinals, however, lose their next six games to drop out of the pennant race. They finish the season October 1 in third place at 86-76.

Sept. 29—Owner **August A. Busch Jr.** dies at age 90. Control of the Cardinals falls to Anheuser-Busch brewery executive Fred Kuhlmann.

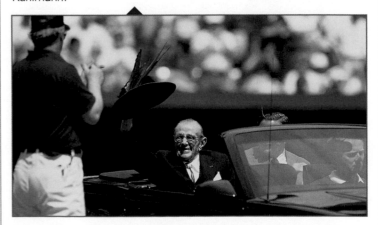

1990

May 4—The Cardinals trade Brunansky to the Red Sox for closer Lee Smith.

June 29—The Cardinals are no-hit, 6-0, in Los Angeles by Dodgers lefthander Fernando Valenzuela. Earlier that night, Oakland's Dave Stewart throws a 5-0 no-hitter against Toronto, marking the first time in the 20th century that two complete-game no-hitters are pitched on the same day.

TORRE

July 6—Herzog, his team in last place at 33-47, resigns after 10 years as manager. Schoendienst succeeds him on an interim basis.

Aug. 1—**Joe Torre** is hired as manager.

Aug. 29—The Cardinals trade McGee to Oakland for three prospects. McGee, who is hitting .335 at the time of the deal, later is awarded the N.L. batting title even though he has one fewer at-bat than the minimum required, since adding one more at-bat without a hit would not drop his average below that of the second-place hitter, Dodgers first baseman Eddie Murray.

Oct. 3—The Cardinals go 70-92 and finish in last place for the first time since 1918.

1991

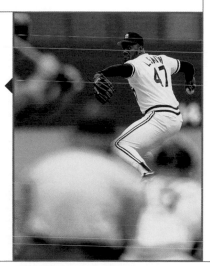

Oct. 2—**Lee Smith** records his 47th save of the season in a 6-4 victory over the Expos at Busch Stadium after breaking Sutter's N.L. record of 45 the day before.

Oct. 6—The Cardinals end the season with a 7-3 loss at Chicago and finish in second place at 84-78.

1992

Apr. 26—Ozzie Smith steals his 500th career base in a 6-0 loss to the Expos at Busch Stadium.

May 26—Ozzie triples in a 5-2 loss to the Dodgers at Busch for career hit No. 2,000.

Sept. 5—Worrell gets career save No. 128 to pass Sutter and become the Cardinals' all-time leader. The next night, Worrell saves a game for starter Bob Tewksbury, who ends the year with the league's best winning percentage (.762), second-best ERA (2.16) and the best walks-per-nine-innings ratio (0.77) of any big-league pitcher since 1933. Tewksbury's won-lost record: 16-5.

Oct. 4—The Cardinals beat the Phillies, 6-3, to finish the season in third place at 83-79.

1993

Apr. 13—Lee Smith passes Jeff Reardon to become baseball's all-time saves leader with No. 358 in a 9-7 victory at Los Angeles.

May 22—Ozzie Smith appears in his 2,223rd game at shortstop, breaking an N.L. record held by Larry Bowa.

Sept. 7—Mark Whiten ties two major league single-game records in the nightcap of a doubleheader in Cincinnati as he hits four homers and drives in 12 runs in a 15-2 St. Louis victory. His homers are a grand slam in the first inning, three-run blasts in the sixth and seventh innings and a two-run shot in the ninth.

Oct. 3—The Cardinals go 87-75 to finish in third place, 10 games behind N.L. East champion Philadelphia.

1994

May 13-14—Ozzie Smith homers in back-to-back games for the only time in his career.

July 14—**Ozzie** gets his 8,017th career assist to pass Luis Aparicio for the top spot on baseball's all-time list for shortstops.

July 18—The Cardinals tie a National League record by blowing an 11-run lead and losing, 15-12, to the Astros in Houston.

July 30—A crowd of 53,415 —the most ever for a regular-season game at Busch Stadium—witnesses a 10-7 Cardinals win over the Cubs. But there's not much at stake —the clubs are tied for fourth place.

Aug. 11—The Cardinals beat the Marlins, 8-6, in Miami in their final game before a players strike wipes out the remainder of the season. The Cardinals finish third in the newly created N.L. Central with a record of 53-61.

1995

June 16—The Cardinals trade third baseman Todd Zeile to the Cubs for three players. Torre is fired after a 20-27 start; farm director Mike Jorgensen takes over as interim manager.

Aug. 10—The Cards get a forfeit win in Los Angeles when Dodgers fans toss that night's promotional giveaway—baseballs—onto the field.

Oct. 1—The 62-81 Cardinals finish in fourth place in the N.L. Central.

Oct. 23—**Tony La Russa** is hired as manager.

Oct. 25—Anheuser-Busch says it will sell the team and Busch Stadium. Two months later, the Cards are bought by a group of local investors headed by Andrew Baur, Fred Hanser and William DeWitt.

1996

Jan.—Busch Stadium has a grass field for the first time since 1969.

Feb. 13—Dennis Eckersley is obtained in a deal with the A's.

May 18—John Mabry is the first Cardinal since Ken Boyer in 1964 to hit for the cycle in order (single, double, triple, home run) but the Cards lose at Colorado, 9-8.

June 19—Ozzie Smith announces his retirement, effective at the end of the season.

Sept. 24—The Cards win their first division

title since 1987 as they beat the Pirates, 7-1, to clinch the N.L. Central. Five days later, they finish at 88-74.

Oct. 5—The Cardinals complete a three-game sweep of the Padres in the N.L. Division Series with a 7-5 victory.

Oct. 13—The Cardinals take a three games-to-one lead over the Braves in the NLCS as they score three runs in the seventh inning of Game 4 to tie it and then win, 4-3, on **Brian Jordan**'s solo homer in the eighth inning in St. Louis. The Cardinals, however, lose the next three games by a combined score of 32-1.

1997

Apr. 19—The Cardinals and Padres take major league baseball to Hawaii. The Cards sweep a doubleheader from San Diego, 1-0 and 2-1, in Honolulu.

June 14—St. Louis splits a day-night doubleheader with the Indians at Busch in the franchise's first interleague play.

July 31—The Cardinals acquire first baseman Mark McGwire from Oakland at the trading deadline.

Aug. 8—In his second at-bat at Busch Stadium, McGwire snaps a string of 71 at-bats without a home run by smashing a 441-foot shot against the Phillies. It is McGwire's first National League homer and the 364th of his career.

Sept. 16—McGwire signs a three-year contract extension and celebrates by hitting a 517-foot homer that evening at Busch.

Sept. 28—The Cardinals finish 73-89 and slip to fourth place.

1998

Mar. 31—McGwire hits the first opening-day grand slam in club history in a 6-0 Cardinals win over the Dodgers at Busch Stadium.

Apr. 14—McGwire is the first Cardinal to have a three-homer game at Busch. His spree comes against Arizona.

May 8—McGwire hits his 400th career homer, connecting off the Mets' Rick Reed at Shea Stadium.

May 16—McGwire clubs the longest homer in Busch Stadium history when he tags Florida's Livan Hernandez for a 545-foot shot. The ball just misses landing in the upper deck in center field.

July 26—McGwire breaks Mize's club record for one season with his 44th homer in a 3-1 victory at Colorado.

Sept. 7—McGwire ties Roger Maris' single-season record when he hits home run No. 61 at Busch Stadium off Chicago righthander Mike Morgan—a 430-foot blast that hits off the Stadium Club windows in left field.

Sept. 8—In the fourth inning of a game against the Cubs—the Cardinals' last home

game before a five-game road swing—**McGwire** makes history by hitting home run No. 62 to become baseball's single-season home run king. The record-breaker is McGwire's shortest homer of the year—a 341-foot line drive off Cubs righthander Steve Trachsel that barely clears the wall down the left field line at Busch Stadium. The Cardinals' J.D. Drew makes his major league debut that night and goes 0-for-2.

Sept. 27—McGwire ends his record season by hitting two more homers—his 69th and 70th of the season—on the final day in a 6-3 win over the Expos at Busch Stadium. The Cardinals finish in third place at 83-79. Due mainly to McGwire, they lead the league in homers (223) for the first time since 1944 and reach three million in attendance for the first time since 1989.

1999

Apr. 23—Third baseman **Fernando Tatis** sets a major league record by hitting two grand slams in the same inning in a 12-5 victory at Dodger Stadium. Both come off Chan Ho Park in the third inning.

June 25—Cardinals rookie Jose Jimenez outduels Randy Johnson—and how. The righthander holds the Diamondbacks hitless and wins, 1-0, at Arizona.

Aug. 5—McGwire hits his 500th career homer, the smash coming against Padres righthander Andy Ashby at Busch Stadium. San Diego's Tony Gwynn, closing in on his 3,000th hit, has one double and ends the game at 2,999.

Oct. 3—The Cardinals close a 75-86 season with a 9-5 win over the Cubs. McGwire finishes the season with 65 homers to lead the majors for a fourth consecutive year.

2000

Apr. 30—McGwire and **Jim Edmonds**—acquired from Anaheim in a March 23 trade—homer in a 4-3 win at Philadelphia as the Cards end the month with an N.L.record-tying 55 homers in April.

July 6—After homering in his first major league at-bat two days earlier, Keith McDonald becomes the first N.L. player to homer in his first two career at-bats in a 12-6 loss to Cincinnati.

July 17—Thirteen days after McDonald homers in his first at-bat, Chris Richard hits the first pitch he sees in the majors (from Twins pitcher Mike Lincoln) over the wall.

July 31—With McGwire injured, the Cardinals acquire veteran first baseman **Will Clark** in a trade with the Orioles.

Sept. 20—The Cardinals clinch their second N.L. Central title in five years with an 11-6 victory over the Astros. St. Louis finishes the season October 1 at 95-67.

Oct. 5—Clark, who hit .345 with 12 homers and 42 RBIs in 171 at-bats for St. Louis during the regular

season, hits a three-run homer in the bottom of the first off Atlanta's Tom Glavine in Game 2 of the Division Series to give the Cardinals a lead they never surrender in a 10-4 victory. The Cards, who had overcome Rick Ankiel's wildness to win Game 1, complete a sweep on Oct. 7.

Oct. 16—The Mets beat the Cardinals, 7-0, in New York to win the NLCS in five games.

2001

Aug. 11—McGwire hits home run No. 574 off Mets lefthander Glendon Rusch to move past Harmon Killebrew for fifth place on the all-time list.

Aug. 29—The Cardinals beat the Padres, 16-14, in the highest-scoring game in Busch Stadium history.

Sept. 3—Rookie lefthander Bud Smith no-hits the Padres, 4-0, in San Diego in his 11th big-league start.

Sept. 17—After six days of inactivity in the wake of the terrorist attacks on the United States, major league baseball resumes play. Broadcaster Jack Buck leads an emotional tribute to America before the Cardinals-Brewers game at Busch Stadium.

Oct. 4—McGwire hits the 583rd and final homer of his career, connecting against the Brewers' Rocky Coppinger in a 10-3 St. Louis win at Milwaukee.

Oct. 7—The Cardinals close the season with a 9-2 loss to the Astros at Busch Stadium to finish tied with Houston for first place in the N.L. Central at 93-69. Because Houston won the season series with St. Louis, the Cardinals qualify for the playoffs as the N.L. wild card.

Oct. 14—The Cardinals are knocked out of the playoffs when Arizona's Tony Womack delivers an RBI single in the bottom of the ninth to beat St. Louis, 2-1, in Game 5 of the Division Series.

Nov. 11—McGwire announces his retirement.

Nov. 12— Outfielder/third baseman/first baseman **Albert Pujols** (.329, 37 homers, 130 RBIs) is unanimously voted N.L. Rookie of the Year. His RBI total is a National League record for a rookie.

2002

Jan. 8—Ozzie Smith, a Cardinal from 1982-96, is elected to the Baseball Hall of Fame.

Apr. 1—The Cardinals pound the Rockies, 10-2, at Busch Stadium on opening day.

May 4—Unknown **Jason Simontacchi**, whose resume included stints in the independent Frontier League and the Italian Professional League, is called up from Memphis and defeats Atlanta, 3-2. He wins his first five decisions.

May 12—Muddling along with a 16-20 record and trailing 8-0 after two innings at Cincinnati, the Cards storm back for a 10-8 victory capped by Drew's two-run home run in the eighth. The stirring win begins a spurt in which St. Louis wins 10 of 11 games.

June 18—After tying for first place in the N.L. Central on June 16, St. Louis takes sole possession of the top spot as Darryl Kile beats the Angels, 7-2. Cardinals broadcaster Jack Buck dies that night.

June 22—Kile is found dead in his Chicago hotel room. That day's Cardinals-Cubs game at Wrigley Field is postponed.

July 28—Trailing the archrival Cubs, 9-4, in the bottom of the ninth inning at Busch Stadium, the Cards strike for six runs. Edgar Renteria 's three-run homer is the game-winner.

July 29—In a blockbuster deal, the Cardinals acquire All-Star third baseman Scott Rolen and a minor league

pitcher from the Phillies in exchange for pitchers Bud Smith and Mike Timlin and infielder Placido Polanco.

July 31—Still shaken over the loss of Buck and Kile, the Cards show remarkable resolve under La Russa and compile a 17-9 record in July. By month's end, they have built a five-game lead in the Central Division.

Sept. 1-29—After cooling off in August (17-14), the Cards go 21-6 in September. They finish 97-65 and win the division by 13 games over Houston. Pujols and Edmonds combine for 62 homers, and Pujols has 127 RBIs. In 55 games, Rolen hits 14 home

runs with 44 RBIs. Morris wins 17 games and Simontacchi 11. Considering retirement after a rough start, Benes goes 5-2 with a 1.86 ERA after the All-Star break.

Oct. 5—The Cards sweep Arizona in the N.L. Division Series, but an injury in Game 2 to Rolen (severe shoulder

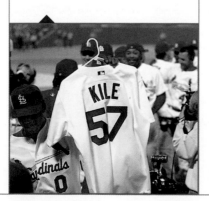

sprain) sidelines the infielder for the rest of the postseason.

Oct. 14—The Giants oust the Cardinals from the NLCS, four games to one, on Kenny Lofton's two-out RBI single in the ninth inning of Game 5.

Nov. 6—St. Louis' La Russa is named the N.L.'s Manager of the Year.

Nov. 14—Cardinals second baseman Fernando Vina, shortstop Renteria, third baseman **Rolen** and center fielder Edmonds win Gold Gloves.

2003

Apr. 2—Woody Williams pitches two-hit ball over 6⅔ innings as the Cards prevail, 7-0, over Milwaukee in the season's second game. Williams goes on to a career-best 18-9 season.

June 12—Injured closer Jason Isringhausen makes his season debut at Boston.

July 13—In the last game before the All-Star break, Pujols is plunked by Padres pitcher Adam Eaton a day after he hits a game-winning homer in the 11th inning. An altercation erupts, with Pujols punching catcher Gary Bennett in the face. Pujols receives a two-game suspension, which he serves in August.

July 15—Pujols and Rolen rank 1-2 in voting for the N.L. All-Star team. They are joined on the squad by fellow starter Renteria, Edmonds and Williams, giving the Cardinals five All-Star team members for the first time since 1985.

Aug. 22—Pujols returns to the lineup after his suspension and a bout with the flu and sees his 30-game hitting streak halted.

ROLEN

Aug. 26—The Cardinals open a three-game series with the Cubs at Busch with a loss but go on to win the next two and tie Houston for the division lead.

Sept. 4—St. Louis loses for the fourth time in a five-game series at Wrigley Field. The Astros, Cubs and Cardinals are now 1-2-3 in the Central race.

Sept. 10—La Russa becomes the eighth major league manager to win 2,000 games as the Cardinals wallop Colorado, 10-2.

Sept. 14—A 4-1 loss to Houston is the Cards' 10th defeat in 14 games in September, putting them 5½ games out of first place with 12 games remaining.

Sept. 26—A 7-6 setback at Arizona eliminates the Cardinals from playoff contention. The team winds up in third place with an 85-77 record.

Sept. 28—In the closest batting race in N.L. history, Pujols edges the Rockies' Todd Helton, .35871 to .35849. Pujols also leads the N.L. in runs (137), hits (212), doubles (51) and total bases (394).

Sept. 28—Catcher Mike Matheny is only the third catcher in big-league history to record a 1.000 fielding percentage.

Oct. 20—Pujols is named Major League Player of the Year by the SPORTING NEWS.

Nov. 4—Shortstop Renteria, third baseman Rolen, center fielder Edmonds and catcher Matheny win Gold Gloves.

2004

April 29—Edmonds hits a walkoff homer in the 13th inning to give the Cards a 5-4 win over the Phillies. The victory makes La Russa only the second manager (Sparky Anderson is the other) to post 700 victories with two teams. La Russa also reached that figure with the A's.

June 11—St. Louis grabs the divisional lead (35-26 record) with a 12-7 interleague win at Texas and holds the top spot the rest of the season.

July 13—Renteria, Pujols and Rolen start for the N.L. in the All-Star Game and go 4-for-7.

Aug. 4—Matheny makes a throwing error against Montreal. It ends the longest errorless streak ever by a catcher, 252 games (covering 1,631 chances).

Aug. 17—Larry Walker, acquired 11 days earlier from Colorado, wallops a grand slam at Busch in a 7-2 victory over Cincinnati.

Sept. 20—The Cards clinch their fourth division title (and third outright crown) in five seasons with a 7-4 win at Milwaukee.

Sept. 26—In a 9-3 romp at Colorado, **Pujols** goes 4-for-5 with his 46th homer and four RBIs. He joins Joe DiMaggio and Ted Williams as the only players to reach 500 RBIs in their first four seasons.

Oct. 3—A 9-4 home victory over the Brewers gives St.

Louis a final 105-57 record. The win total is the highest for the franchise since 1944 and tops in the majors in '04.

Oct. 10—The Cardinals win the Division Series against Los Angeles, three games to one.

Oct. 20-21—Edmonds puts his stamp on the Cardinals' NLCS win over the Astros, first with a game-winning home run in the 12th inning of Game 6, then with a diving catch to save two runs in the second inning of Game 7. His momentum-changing defensive play helps the Cards beat Houston and Roger Clemens, 5-2, and notch their 16th N.L. pennant.

Oct. 27—The Red Sox complete a four-game World Series sweep of the Cardinals for their first Series title in 86 years.

2005

Apr. 8—The Cardinals win the final home opener in the stadium, overcoming a 5-1 deficit and defeating the Phillies, 6-5, on consecutive bases-loaded walks in the eighth inning. New shortstop David Eckstein reaches base five times.

Apr. 23—**Mark Mulder**, another newcomer, outpitches Houston's Clemens, going the distance in a 1-0, 10-inning victory.

Apr. 27—Mark Grudzielanek becomes the third Cardinal to hit for the cycle at Busch (Brock and Ray Lankford are the others). Chris Carpenter strikes out 12 Brewers in a 6-3 win as the Cards improve to 14-5.

May 2—St. Louis, down 9-3 at

Cincinnati, strikes for seven ninth-inning runs and wins, 10-9. Edmonds hits a three-run homer in the ninth and Mabry delivers the winning two-run shot.

May 10—Scott Rolen injures his shoulder in a collision with Dodgers first baseman Hee Seop Choi.

June 25—Carpenter pitches his third shutout as the Cards (47-27) stop Pittsburgh, 8-0.

July 7—Catcher Yadier Molina suffers a broken left hand when hit by a pitch from Arizona's Claudio Vargas.

July 10—N.L. Central leader St. Louis is 56-32 at the All-Star break, leads second-place Houston by 11½ games.

July 12—N.L. manager La Russa names Carpenter to start the All-Star Game. He's joined in the starting lineup by Eckstein, Pujols and Edmonds. Rolen is voted the starter at third but pulls out to rest his shoulder. Isringhausen also is

on the N.L. squad. Carpenter works one inning, giving up two hits but no runs.

July 18—Outfielder Reggie Sanders (leg fracture) is placed on the disabled list. Rolen joins the D.L. four days later because of his still-ailing shoulder, and Walker is added on July 26 with a neck injury.

Aug. 4—The team announces KTRS will become its flagship radio station beginning in 2006, ending a 52-season association with KMOX.

Aug. 5—Pujols homers against Atlanta and becomes the first player in major league history to hit 30 or

more home runs in each of his first five seasons.

Aug. 7—**Eckstein**'s ninth-inning grand slam enables the Cardinals to steal a 5-3 home

victory over the Braves.

Aug. 19—The Cards trail the Giants, 4-0, entering the bottom of the ninth. Molina, in his second game back after recovering from his hand injury, drills a three-run homer and Edmonds hits a two-run double with two out to win it.

Aug. 21—Rolen opts for season-ending shoulder surgery.

Aug. 31—Pujols joins Al Simmons, Ted Williams and Joe DiMaggio as the only players to reach the 100-RBI plateau in each of their first five big-league seasons.

Sept. 3—Carpenter, matched against fellow Cy Young Award candidate Clemens, beats Houston for his 20th victory.

Sept. 13—The Cards soar to 40 games over .500 (93-53).

Sept. 17—Two days after clinching the N.L. Central crown because of a tiebreaker edge, the Cardinals win the division outright by defeating the Cubs, 5-1, at Wrigley Field. They go on to finish 100-62.

Oct. 8—The Cards sweep San Diego in the Division Series.

Oct. 17—A strike away from NLCS elimination in Game 5 and down two runs, the Cardinals get two men on base ahead of Pujols, who stuns the Astros and their fans with a monster game-winning homer. But Houston wins Game 6 and the N.L. pennant two nights later.

PUJOLS